TIKI *with a* TWIST

TIKI with a

TWIST

75 FRESH, COOL, AND WILD TROPICAL COCKTAILS

Lynn Calvo
WITH JAMES O. FRAIOLI

FOREWORD BY JOHN SHEA

PHOTOGRAPHY BY KAREN WISE AT LYNN'S HULA HUT

STERLING EPICURE

New York

STERLING EPICURE
New York

An Imprint of Sterling Publishing Co., Inc.
1166 Avenue of the Americas
New York, NY 10036

One recipe in this book contains part of a raw egg. Consuming raw or undercooked eggs
may increase your risk of foodborne illness. The young, elderly, pregnant women, and
anyone who may be immunocompromised should not consume them.

ISBN 978-1-4549-1826-4

Distributed in Canada by Sterling Publishing Co., Inc.
c/o Canadian Manda Group, 664 Annette Street,
Toronto, Ontario, M6S 2C8, Canada
Distributed in the United Kingdom by GMC Distribution Services
Castle Place, 166 High Street, Lewes, East Sussex, BN7 1XU, United Kingdom
Distributed in Australia by Capricorn Link (Australia) Pty. Ltd.
P.O. Box 704, Windsor, NSW 2756, Australia

For information about custom editions, special sales, and premium and corporate
purchases, please contact Sterling Special Sales at 800-805-5489
or specialsales@sterlingpublishing.com.

Manufactured in Canada

2 4 6 8 10 9 7 5 3 1

www.sterlingpublishing.com

A complete list of photo credits appears on page 173

Design by Lorie Pagnozzi.

TO MY FATHER, JOHN, AND MY MOTHER, MILLY,
FOR THEIR ENDLESS LOVE AND SUPPORT
AND BECAUSE THEY ALWAYS SAID,
"NEVER GO STRAIGHT, ALWAYS GO FORWARD."

Contents

From left to right: Hot Pink Drink,
Montauk Marine Cooler, Bourbon Bash,
Great White Bite, Rosemary Lemonade

Foreword

WHILE IN MONTAUK, at the eastern end of Long Island, I stumbled across a heavenly slice of tropical paradise: Lynn's Hula Hut, complete with a waterfront location and colorful locals. I immediately fell in love with two of the handcrafted cocktail surprises: the Brazilian Breezer and the Very Berry Brazil. These clever drinks are the real thing: infused with herbs, fruit, vegetables, and lots of love.

Beautiful, bold, and bohemian, the Hula Hut experience is the creation of Lynn Calvo, a successful entrepreneur, who has traveled the globe in her quest to develop exciting exotic concoctions, which she graciously shares with visitors who have discovered her tiki oasis, just as I did. I sauntered past swaying palms into the embrace of the bamboo hut, and, as her lovely liquid creations hit my lips, I found myself transported to a faraway island, someplace I'd only dreamed of. Yet I opened my eyes to an equally amazing destination: friendly faces gathered around a tropical bar buzzing with activity. On the beach, a local band strummed guitars, inviting patrons to dance the night away on the sand. Aromas of ripe fruit and fresh herbs—keys ingredients in Lynn's refreshing cocktails—lingered as rifts of blues, reggae, or rock 'n' roll drifted across the water, luring others to join the fun. It's easy to get lost among the good people there, as though you've been invited to an exclusive beach party. With her charming, confident personality, Lynn sashayed through the crowd, encouraging artists, businesspeople, fishermen, stylish New Yorkers, and international travelers to drink, dance, and unwind in the Zen Den or in a hammock as flickering torches welcomed the night.

Many of history's original tiki drinks are unforgettable, made with rare infused liquors, served in iconic ceramic mugs filled with homemade juices and adorned with gorgeous fruits and flowers. They're happiness in a glass, and you'll find a selection of those original drinks, along with Lynn's clever twists on them, in this book, which is a magic carpet: read it and learn to fly. Sipping the Hukilau Lemonade will transport you to Maui. Shake up the Boudreaux's Bayou Berry Tea, and you'll dance at dawn on Bourbon Street. A few days ago, the Mellow Yellow put me on a beach in Tahiti.

Tiki culture is fun anywhere you go but particularly in Montauk, an unlikely place to find it. Lynn has perfected a sophisticated yet playful twist on all things tiki, and I can't wait to return for more. Until I do, I'll enjoy this beautiful book of amazing, creative recipes that she's gathered here for all of us to enjoy.

Bottoms up, tops off, and here's to the good life!

—JOHN SHEA, EMMY AWARD—WINNING ACTOR AND DIRECTOR

Introduction

WHEN I WAS A CHILD, my Grandpa Angelo, a World War II veteran, proudly displayed the hula girl tattoo emblazoned on the inside of his right forearm. "Make her dance!" I often cried. He flexed, and away she went.

Many servicemen, including my grandfather and James Michener, returned from the war with romantic stories of the South Seas. As a result, the Polynesian presence in Western pop culture soared. Michener's tales served as the inspiration for *South Pacific*, the Rodgers and Hammerstein musical that premiered on Broadway in 1949. But a decade and a half beforehand, Louisiana native Ernest Gantt had unveiled Don's Beachcomber Cafe, America's first Polynesian-themed restaurant, in Hollywood. Soon after, Victor Bergeron opened the doors of the first Trader Vic's® location. Debate raged between the two men over who had invented the infamous Mai Tai®, but the tiki craze flourished, and other popular drinks, such as the Zombie and the Scorpion Bowl, soon shared the limelight.

The Polynesian influence on American pop culture peaked during the 1950s, making its mark on architecture, cuisine, and music—particularly the Martin Denny Orchestra. Denny, an American composer, became known as the father of Exotica, a musical genre that celebrates tiki culture and combines the musical traditions of far-away tropical locales: bongos, congas, and Cuban jazz rhythms. Les Baxter, Juan García Esquivel, and Arthur Lyman also composed Exotica music, and you can hear their work in the soundtracks of many movies of that period. Tropical mania waned for a time, but the tiki craze has returned. Today, the revitalized Polynesian vibe is going strong as Old Spice® or the Twinkie. Tribal tattoos, backyard bars, and fruity cocktails abound.

But years ago in the Caribbean, when Cruzan rum sold for $1.89 a liter and islanders regarded clothing as optional, my friends and I hoisted our dinghy ashore on Necker Island in the British Virgin Islands. To our delight, goats ran freely, but the tiki bar that we found—a hidden gem off the beaten path—excited us more. It wasn't much more than a wooden shack that two brothers had pirated from a neighboring island. One of them flashed a machete, smiled, and went about chopping the fresh coconuts that he had harvested moments earlier. He handed the carved fruit to his brother, who filled the nuts with rum and fresh lime juice. It was pure heaven. Sadly, Necker

Island has become an exclusive resort, but it will always remain part of the inspiration for Lynn's Hula Hut, another story I'm proud to share with you.

After years in the restaurant and design business in Colorado, I returned to Montauk to begin a new chapter of my life. For those unfamiliar, Montauk lies at the easternmost tip of Long Island and is known for its temperate climate and an abundance of farms and vineyards. As you head east from Manhattan, the hustle and bustle of the city gradually fades along the 120-mile drive into a scenic stretch along a two-lane road that passes through the Hamptons, a series of small seaside hamlets. Farther east, quaint towns give way to long stretches of sandy beaches, summer resorts, and breathtaking glimpses of the Atlantic Ocean. My heart still flutters at the first sight of the sea. Most of us refer to Montauk as "the End." The Native Americans and early Dutch settlers called it "the promised land" on account of its rich soil and the abundance of local seafood. I spent my childhood summers here with my mother and my father, a handsome, rugged lobsterman with a great sense of humor. A tight-knit Italian family, we shared our home with my grandparents, and my fondest childhood memories are of fishing and clamming with my father and helping Grandma Fiorita in her garden.

Returning to Montauk as an adult, I bought a long-bed pickup truck and converted it into a mobile tiki bar to cater private events throughout the Hamptons. It was my new calling, but it wasn't my first time slinging drinks here. A tavern owner had tried to reassure me—at the tender age of 18 and with absolutely no training—"Don't worry, this is a beer and shot bar. It won't be busy. All the fishermen are out at sea."

A nor'easter promptly blew in, just my luck, and the bar filled to the gills. The money was great, but it was just a job then. When I came back, having my own bar gave me a purpose. It became my dream, and the challenges ahead felt exciting. I had my mobile tiki bar painted Sunset Orange Effect, a bona fide midcentury modern color. Large hibiscus flowers graced the sides, and my slogan, HAVE TIKI, WILL TRAVEL, accentuated the door panels. A custom teak bar topped with a large thatched palapa covered the truck bed and provided an authentic island feel.

In 2010, my dear friend Carl Darenberg asked me to set up my tiki truck bar at his marina for an upcoming shark tournament. My tropical cocktails were a hit, so I asked Carl about setting up something more permanent.

"My dad tried for years," he replied, "but the town wouldn't let him."

That didn't make sense. Marinas all over the world have dockside bars. I asked Carl whether he'd lease me a spot in the parking lot if I could get the zoning changed and a marina bar approved. He laughed but agreed. After two and a half arduous years, three different site plans, numerous applications, and thousands of dollars, my little slice of paradise finally opened for business.

Today, Lynn's Hula Hut is Montauk's tropical oasis. "The Hut," as locals call it, stands on the edge of the harbor, adorned with bamboo siding and surrounded by sugar-white beach sand and large swaying palms. The air smells of the sea—as well as mint, basil, and cilantro from my herb garden, which provides fresh leaves for my Pacific Rim–inspired purees and cocktails. Music always plays, sometimes reggae, Cuban jazz, or a bluesy riff. On the bar deck stools, the oversized bamboo couch, or the cozy chairs in the sand, you can enjoy a few cold tiki drinks with friends, share stories, and relax in the sunshine. If you prefer something a little more low key, you can retreat to the Hammock Garden, a peaceful, shady retreat known as the Zen Den by day (and the Boom Boom Room after sunset). A large Buddha serenely welcomes you as wind chimes dance above your head, creating a delicate melody.

Here my love of design and mixology come together. It's also the place where I met my friend and coauthor, James O. Fraioli, a television producer and award-winning author of dozens of beautiful cookbooks, including one that garnered a coveted James Beard Award in 2014. We immediately bonded over our shared passions for great food, exotic cocktails, and a fresh-is-best philosophy. Our fun, fresh, lighthearted book encourages you to escape, if only for an hour, to some faraway island brimming with sunshine, rum, and sparkling water. Let's toast to finding your own tropical paradise, wherever it may lie, while you soak up the sun and fill yourself with inspiration to create your own tiki cocktails to enjoy with loved ones on that sandy beach someplace—even if it's in your own backyard.

paper parasols ·······

straws ·······

skewers ·······

Tools of the Trade

Whether you're a professional mixologist or a backyard bartender, having the right bar tools is essential. I love to shop in thrift stores and hunt for vintage barware, like leather-bound ice buckets and unique glassware, for hosting parties. You can never have too many vintage tiki mugs, midcentury modern Collins glasses, or decanters. Attention-grabbing cocktail trays are a great way to serve your favorite concoctions—as is wearing a vintage cocktail apron. Beginners should start with a local restaurant or bar supply store. Here's what you need to get started.

BLENDER

A stick or immersion blender is fine for liquids, but always use a countertop model when blending ice, and *always* secure the lid before turning it on. It sounds like a basic step, but you'll be unpleasantly surprised if that lid is loose!

BOTTLES

Use decorative glass bottles fitted with pour spouts to store and serve your syrups.

CONTAINERS

For your purees, use plastic squeeze bottles, which you can find online or at restaurant supply stores—and buy them new. You don't want your tropical cocktails tasting sour!

CUTTING BOARD

Wood is good, but plastic works, too.

ICE BUCKET AND TONGS

An insulated bucket with a lid will keep your ice from melting on hot summer days.

JIGGER

Two-sided jiggers run the gamut of sizes. Invest in a good one that delineates a variety of fractions.

JUICER

Invest in a good-quality electric model. You're going to be juicing a lot of fruit, so it's worth the money.

KNIFE

I prefer one with a medium-size, nonserrated blade, such as a kitchen knife or chef's knife. Whatever kind you use, make sure it's sharp. A dull knife is more dangerous than a sharp one because it will slip more easily.

MUDDLER

This handheld rod with a flat, rounded bottom is used to extract herbal essences and crush fruits and other ingredients in the bottom of a glass. Again, wood is good, but plastic works, too.

PAPER PARASOLS

These are not strictly tools, but a must-have for that true island feel.

PEELER

A Y-shaped peeler gives you more control and cleaner twists, but in a pinch you can use the vegetable peeler that you already have in your kitchen drawer.

POUR SPOUT

Spring for the ones with built-in screens, which will keep fruit flies out of your syrups and spirits.

SHAKER

I prefer a cobbler shaker, which consists of three interlocking stainless steel pieces: the cup, the strainer, and the cap. You can also use a mixing glass and a Hawthorne strainer.

SKEWERS

Short ones, about 4 inches, made of bamboo are great for garnishes.

STRAINER

If you make your drinks with a shaker that doesn't have a built-in strainer, make sure you either have a Hawthorne strainer on hand, which has a curved metal coil that allows you to adjust the level of the strain, or a julep strainer, which is bowl-shaped and slotted with small holes through which liquid can pass. There are a lot of cheap strainers on the market, most with loose springs that easily fall off. Look for a strainer that has some weight, doesn't feel flimsy, and has a nice tight and sturdy coil.

STRAWS

The more colorful and exotic the better!

shaker

jigger

tongs

julep strainer

ice bucket ⊢⊣⊢⊣⊢⊣⊢⊣⊢⊣⊢⊣⊢⊣⊢⊣⊢⊣⊢⊣⊢

mason jar

snifter

coconut shell

Glassware & Serving Vessels

The glass, cup, or bowl in which you serve a drink is quite literally its foundation. Selecting one with the right size and shape is important. Each has its reason and purpose.

COCONUT SHELL

Making these from scratch will look great but takes a lot of time and effort. If you can't find them in a local store, it's better to buy them online.

COLLINS GLASS

A tall, cylindrical glass that holds between 8 and 14 ounces.

COUPE

Supposedly molded from Marie Antoinette's left breast, this old-fashioned Champagne glass now used for modern cocktails holds around 5 or 6 ounces. Chill in the freezer in advance.

FLUTE

With a tall, narrow bowl on a stem, this glass that holds between 4 and 6 ounces is the preferred serving vessel for sparkling wine.

HIGHBALL

Named for a railroad instrument that indicated speed, this is a cross between a Collins glass and a rocks glass that holds from 8 to 12 ounces

HURRICANE GLASS

Resembling a glass-footed hurricane lantern, it can hold 12 to 20 ounces.

MARGARITA GLASS

An enlarged, modified coupe that can hold anywhere from 8 to 16 ounces.

MARTINI GLASS

A V-shaped glass with a long stem typically used to serve chilled and strained cocktails ranging from 6 to 12 ounces. Chill in the freezer in advance.

MASON JAR

A glass jar, with glass screw threads around the neck for a metal lid, that can hold 8 to 16 ounces

PILSNER GLASS

A Collins glass with sass that tapers inward toward the bottom and holds between 8 and 12 ounces.

PINT GLASS

A 16-ounce glass either in an inverted conical shape or the nonik (pronounced "no-Nick") variety, which swells outward toward the top.

ROCKS GLASS

A short, cylindrical glass that holds between 6 and 8 ounces. Large rocks glasses can hold up to 10 or 12 ounces.

SNIFTER

A short round bowl that has a narrow mouth and a glass foot that can hold around 6 or 8 ounces.

TIKI BOWLS

Tiki bowls were and still are designed by tiki artists for those seeking a much larger ceramic vessel in which to serve more than 36 ounces of liquor for two or more people to share. The scorpion bowl is one such example. Other bowls—which often showcase artistic designs of Hawaiian and Polynesian villages, oceans, and gods emblazoned on the sides—can hold volumes over 52 ounces and satisfy the communal thirst of four or more adults. The volcano bowl is large enough to tackle this task and comes with a built-in crater in the center, into which goes a small pool of overproof rum, such as Bacardi® 151, that you carefully can ignite to create volcanic ambience. There's nothing like sipping an oversize tropical libation through straws with friends amid a glowing flame!

TIKI MUGS

These artful ceramic drink vessels are a must-have when serving classic tiki cocktails. They come in a variety of colors, shapes, and sizes and are fun to use and display. Believed to be created at Don the Beachcomber®, one of America's original tiki bars, tiki drinkware had its heyday in the 1960s and carried through the '80s and '90s when tiki and tropical-themed restaurants like Trader Vic's readily sold their mugs as souvenirs when they weren't filling them with tropical concoctions. Often depicting traditional Polynesian carvings and gods, the iconic tiki mug appeared in all sorts of styles from basic coconuts and pineapples to headhunters, spirits, skulls, hula girls, and rum barrels. You can find original vintage mugs today by scouring swap meets, garage sales, and websites such as eBay. Replicas and new tiki mugs are readily available online.

tiki mug

rocks glass

flute

pint glass

collins glass

Ingredients & Garnishes

Selecting the proper base spirit for making your cocktails as well as infusing garnishes is important. Try not to resort to using cheap alcohol in either case. The quality of the liquor affects the quality of the flavor profile and the garnish and therefore the overall finished cocktail.

When experimenting with flavor-packed modifiers, such as bitters and syrups, always start with smaller amounts. Even those small amounts can alter the flavor profile of a drink quickly and drastically. You can always add more, but you can't take it out once you've poured it in.

Garnishes usually, though not exclusively, consist of slices, spears, twists, wedges, wheels, or whole pieces of fruit or sprigs, leaves, and sometimes blooms of herbs, edible flowers, and other tasty delights. Use your imagination, and remember that garnishes are meant to enhance the flavor of a cocktail and add visual appeal. Many cocktails can be served with one or more garnishes, while some are best left unadorned. If you decide to garnish, use fresh fruits and clean them thoroughly before use. Below you'll find some of the garnishes mentioned later in the book and directions on how to prepare them.

I often use the phrase tiki couture to refer to dressing or styling a cocktail. The right look sets the mood for a gathering, evokes a particular feeling or memory for your guests, and pleases the senses. Don't be afraid to get creative and tap into the inspiration around you. You'd never put your cufflinks or earrings on before you picked out your outfit, so once you've made your drinks, use colorful straws, cocktail umbrellas, edible flowers, and other items to help you "accessorize" and put your signature on each cocktail you serve.

BERRIES

The fresher the berry, the better. Whether you use blackberries, blueberries, raspberries, or strawberries, always remove and discard the stems and leaves; then wash them thoroughly under cold running water before muddling, slicing, garnishing, or serving.

CHERRIES

When soaking cherries in liquor, keep in mind that they're quite dense and take significantly longer to infuse—approximately 2 to 3 weeks—than other softer fruits such as the Drunken Pineapple Wedges (page 21), which take only 2 to 3 days.

Boudreaux's Bourbon Cherry Bomb

1 pint cherries, stems on

1 pint Maker's Mark®, Bulleit®, or other premium bourbon

Fill a large mason jar with the cherries. Add the bourbon, secure the lid tightly, and store in a cool, dry place for 2 to 3 weeks. Makes approximately 1 pint.

Traverse City Cherry Bomb

A trip to Michigan inspired this recipe for rum-soaked cherries. I've never tasted more delicious cherries than the ones I had in Traverse City.

1 pint cherries, stems on

½ pint premium light rum

½ pint premium dark rum

Fill a large mason jar with the cherries, and add both rums. Secure the lid tightly, and turn the jar over several times to blend the rums. Let the cherries soak in a cool, dry place for 2 to 3 weeks. Makes approximately 1 pint.

One evening, a certain well-known country singer from Nashville showed up at Lynn's Hula Hut with his guitar. After most of our guests had gone home, he surprised us with a private concert. A couple of tunes and a couple of drinks later he loudly and proudly proclaimed himself a rough-and-tumble whiskey-drinkin' Southern boy with a high tolerance for bourbon and moonshine. So I offered him a Boudreaux's Bourbon Cherry Bomb, named after my crazy Cajun friend from southern Louisiana.

"Is that all you've got?" he hollered.

So I opened up the mason jar, pulled out a couple more cherries, and shouted back: "Open up, and come to mama!"

Four Cherry Bombs and several songs later, we called his driver and sent him off in true Montauk style.

CITRUS TWIST

Thoroughly rinse the fruit in warm water, and place it on its side on your cutting board. With a sharp knife, slice through the center of the fruit, exposing the flower-shaped center. Slice the halves into wheels ⅛-inch to ¼-inch wide, then slice through the rind and cut off the pulp to leave a long, thin strip of rind. Twist the rind into a coil.

If you have a channel knife (available at most kitchen or restaurant supply stores), you can do this quickly and easily, but be sure to cut the strip of rind off the fruit and twist it directly above the glass so that the flavorful oils from the zest spritz into your cocktail.

CITRUS WEDGE

Thoroughly rinse the fruit in warm water, and place it on its side on your cutting board. Using light pressure, roll the fruit on the board with your hand to soften the pulp inside. Then, with a sharp knife, slice off the ends of the fruit. Align your knife lengthwise with the two cut ends of the fruit, and slice it in half. Turn each half flat side down, align your knife lengthwise again with the two cut ends, and slice in half. Turn each quarter flat side down, align your knife lengthwise one more time with the two cut ends, and slice in half. Cover with a damp paper towel, and refrigerate for up to 24 hours before serving.

CITRUS WHEEL

Thoroughly rinse the fruit in warm water, and place it on its side on your cutting board. With a sharp knife, slice off the ends of the fruit to expose the flower-shaped center. Align your knife lengthwise with the two cut ends of the fruit, and slice halfway through, creating what will be the notch in each wheel that straddles the edge of the glass. Starting at one end, slice the fruit into wheels ⅛-inch to ¼-inch wide. Cover with a damp paper towel, and refrigerate for up to 24 hours before serving.

CUCUMBER SPEAR

Thoroughly rinse the cucumber in warm water. You can leave the skin on or use a peeler to remove some of it to create stripes. Slice off the ends, align your knife lengthwise to the two cut ends, and slice it in half. Turn each half flat side down, align your knife with the ends again, and slice in half again. Turn each quarter flat side down, align your knife with the ends, and slice in half again. Place the spears in a shallow dish or tall glass, cover with water, and refrigerate for up to 24 hours before serving.

CUCUMBER WHEEL

Thoroughly rinse the cucumber in warm water. You can leave the skin on or use a peeler to remove some of it to create stripes. Slice off the ends and, starting at one end, slice the fruit

juicer

into wheels ⅛-inch to ¼-inch wide. Lay each wheel flat, and make a slice from the center through one edge to create the notch that straddles the edge of the glass. Place in a bowl, cover with water, and refrigerate for up to 24 hours before serving.

EDIBLE FLOWERS

You can find edible flowers, such as orchids and hibiscus, at local farmers markets when in season or online at specialty retailers, such as GourmetSweetBotanicals.com or MarxFoods .com. Both sites ship overnight for maximum freshness. Rinse the flowers gently in cold water, and let them air dry on a paper towel. Use them immediately, or store them in an airtight container in the refrigerator for up to 3 or 4 days. Make sure you order 100 percent edible flowers such as hibiscus, jasmine, lavender, lemon verbena, and nasturtiums. They'll make a beautiful statement when used as garnish.

HERBS

Basil, cilantro, mint, and rosemary all grow in an herb garden at the Hula Hut, and all make a wonderful addition to tropical cocktails. Always use fresh herbs, which are much more fragrant and add more depth to a drink than those expensive dried herbs in glass jars. Fresh herbs are relatively easy to grow outside in the summer or inside in a potted container near a windowsill in the winter. You'll find basil, cilantro, dill, lavender, mint, rosemary, sage, thyme, and more in the pages of this book. If you can't grow them yourself, you can always pick them up fresh at your local grocery store or farmers market.

ICE

Size matters when it comes to ice. Use extra large cubes in a rocks glass when serving premium liquors on the rocks, standard or medium-size cubes for drinks served in Collins or highball glasses, and crushed ice for most tropical concoctions. If you don't have a refrigerator that will make crushed ice for you, place the cubes in a sealable plastic freezer bag, and make sure the bag is completely sealed. Smash the cubes with a mallet, meat tenderizer, or other appropriate kitchen tool until the cubes break into small chips.

KIWI WHEEL

Thoroughly rinse the kiwi in warm water, and place it on its side on a cutting surface. Slice off the ends of the fruit, and then slice it in half between the cut ends to expose the starburst center of the fruit. Slice the halves into wheels ⅛-inch to ¼-inch wide. If you prefer to use them skinless, trim the skin from around the wheels. (It's much easier than trying to peel the skin from the whole fruit while trying to hold on to it.) Lay each wheel flat, and make a slice from the center through one edge of the wheel to create the notch that straddles the edge of the glass. Cover with a damp paper towel, and refrigerate for up to 12 hours before serving.

JUICE

Always squeeze all your juices fresh. If I catch you with a store-bought plastic squeeze bottle of flavored water, I'll confiscate it!

LEMONS, LIMES, AND ORANGES

It's always a good idea to have a few fresh lemons, limes, and oranges readily available for spontaneous events or surprise guests. Citrus fruits release more juice when warm, so soak them in warm water for 10 to 15 minutes, or microwave them for 15 to 20 seconds on high, before use.

MANGOS

A healthy, ripe mango should be plump with a light green to reddish-yellow colored skin, depending on the variety. When you pick it up, it should feel heavier than it looks. It's ripe if the skin indents slightly when you squeeze it with your fingers, and it also should have a fruity fragrance. If only unripe mangos are available, leave them on your kitchen counter (better if near sunlight or a window), and they'll ripen in a few days. If the mango has pronounced brown marks or feels mushy, it's too ripe.

MANGO SPEAR

Some grocery stores carry mango spears already prepared and ready to use. They're fresh, delicious, and a great time saver. If yours doesn't, here's how to make them.

Rinse the mango thoroughly in warm water, and stand it on its end on your cutting board. With a peeler or sharp paring knife, slice off the skin, working your way around the fruit. The mango is an oval-shaped fruit with a large, flat pit in the middle, so when holding it on its end, you'll see that it has two wide sides and two narrow sides. Slice down through the mango toward the center along one of the wide sides. If your knife hits the seed, move it slightly away from the center, and continue slicing. Cut as big a single piece as you can. Repeat on the other side, and slice off the fruit that remains on the two narrow sides. Cut the large pieces lengthwise into slices ½-inch to ¾-inch wide. Cover with a damp paper towel, and refrigerate for up to 24 hours before serving. You also can place the spears in a tall jar, cover them with mango nectar, and refrigerate for up to 1 week.

MELONS

Melons are the sweet, fleshy fruit of a plant that originated in southwest Asia and Africa, and they reportedly were grown by European settlers in America as early as the 1600s. Many different varieties are widely available today, including cantaloupe, honeydew, and the summertime favorite watermelon. They all make a delicious garnish.

CANTALOUPE OR HONEYDEW WEDGE

Thoroughly rinse the melon in warm water, and place it on its side on your cutting board. Slice it in half from one end to the other. Using a spoon, scrape the seeds from the center of the fruit and discard them. Lay each half flat side down, and slice in half from end to end again. Place each quarter rind side down, and slice in half from end to end one more time. Slice each piece into 2-inch wedges by cutting through the flesh and just into the rind, making sure not to cut all the way through. Separate the wedges from the rind by slicing between the fruit and the rind from end to end. Cover with a damp paper towel, and refrigerate for up to 24 hours before serving.

WATERMELON WEDGE

Thoroughly rinse a seedless watermelon in warm water, and place it on its side on your cutting board. Slice it in half from end to end. Lay each half flat side down, and slice in half from end to end again. Place each quarter rind side down, and slice in half from end to end

one more time. Slice each piece into wedges 1 to 2 inches wide by cutting through the flesh and just into the rind, making sure not to cut all the way through. Separate the wedges from the rind by slicing between the fruit and the rind from end to end. Cover with a damp paper towel, and refrigerate for up to 24 hours before serving.

MELON BALLS

Thoroughly rinse your melon of choice in warm water, and place it on its side on your cutting board. Slice it in half from end to end. For cantaloupe, honeydew, and other varieties with seeds in the center, use a spoon to scrape out the seeds and discard them. With a melon baller or small ice cream scoop, scoop out the flesh until only the rind remains. Cover with a damp paper towel, and refrigerate for up to 24 hours before serving.

PINEAPPLES

Despite its origin in parts of inland Central America, the pineapple is considered one of the most Polynesian of tropical fruits. Over time, this excellent fruit has served as a staple of native feasts and trade with Europeans and as a universal symbol of celebration and hospitality. If you look carefully, you'll see the symbol used in architecture and design on banisters, door knockers, and elsewhere. Any tiki-themed event or gathering should feature a few symbolic pineapples to welcome guests and set the mood.

This delicious fruit explodes with sweet, juicy flavor when eaten, and it is an excellent source of antioxidants, vitamins (A, B complex, and C), and minerals. Per serving, it has roughly the same number of calories as an apple, and it makes a colorful, versatile garnish or appetizer for any event.

After a pineapple is picked, it doesn't continue to ripen as many other fleshy fruits do. These four tips will help you pick a fresh, sweet, and juicy pineapple every time.

1. A ripe pineapple will have well-developed and relatively flat eyes—the spiked, rough circles making up the geometric pattern on the rind.

2. A fresh pineapple has healthy green leaves and golden-yellow skin. Some light green coloring near the stem is okay. If the leaves are more brown than green or if the skin is reddish-brown, wrinkled, cracked, or moldy, keep looking.

3. The juicier the pineapple, the heavier it will feel. A ripe one will feel firm but give slightly beneath your fingers when you squeeze it. Also try plucking a leaf from the top to check for ripeness. If it comes out with no resistance, the pineapple may be rotten.

4. Ripe pineapples have a sweet scent. If the fruit has no scent, it's not ripe. If it smells of vinegar or alcohol, then it's overripe.

PINEAPPLE WEDGE

For my garnishes, I prefer to leave the skin and core, which takes less time and looks more organic and traditional.

Rinse the pineapple thoroughly in warm water, and place it on its side on your cutting board. Slice off the base and the leaves. If you want to remove the skin, set the pineapple on its base, and slice off the skin, sawing downward and working your way around the fruit. To remove any remaining eyes, cut a V-shaped groove diagonally down each row, again working your way around the fruit. Lay the pineapple on its side, align your knife perpendicular to the two ends, and cut it in half. Place each half flat side down, align your knife perpendicular to the two ends again, and cut it into quarters. Stand each quarter on its end, and slice downward to remove the woody core (optional). Lay each quarter on its side, and slice it into wedges ½-inch to ¾-inch wide. Make a 1-inch cut through the "core point" of each wedge for straddling the edge of a glass. Cover with a damp paper towel, and refrigerate for up to 48 hours before serving.

Drunken Pineapple Wedges

This is my favorite garnish, which I also serve hot off the grill to get the party started. It's great on skewers with coconut curried shrimp or chicken or served over ice cream with bananas. However you prefer them, they're always a big hit.

1 pineapple

½ pint coconut rum

½ pint premium spiced rum

2 tablespoons freshly ground cinnamon

Wash the pineapple thoroughly and cut it into ½-inch-thick wedges, leaving the skin on. Fill a large mason jar with the wedges, add the rums, and then add the cinnamon to taste. Secure the lid tightly, and turn the jar over several times to blend the rums and spice. Let the pineapple soak in a cool dry place for 2 to 3 days.

RUM

Ah, yes, that distilled tropical beverage made from sweet sugarcane and molasses. It's been the go-to spirit for pirates, buccaneers, and the navies of various empires that once sailed through the Caribbean. It's also one of the most frequently featured liquors in tiki cocktails.

Today, many countries around the globe, including the United States, produce rum, although rum connoisseurs proclaim that the best rums still come from the Caribbean and the southern hemisphere, where the majority of the world's rum production still takes place. Rum is available in different grades, from light to gold to dark, all used in cocktail making. More expensive premium rums typically are reserved for sipping neat or over ice. As with any high-priced, top-shelf liquor, you shouldn't mix a fine artisanal rum; that's what the less expensive rums are for.

Some rums are spiced (such as Sailor Jerry™), flavored, or overproof (like Bacardi 151). Note that, when substituting these "altered" rums in a cocktail recipe, you'll change the flavor profile of the drink—for better . . . or for worse! For recipes that simply call for "rum," stick to a traditional rum, and reserve rum variations for recipes that specify when to use a spiced, flavored, or overproof rum.

Syrups

Syrups don't just add sweetness to a cocktail. They can balance bitter or acidic drinks and enhance flavor profiles in a variety of subtle but important ways. It truly is simple: heat equal parts sugar and water until the sugar dissolves. Easier yet, if your home's boiler or water heater is strong enough, pour the hot water and sugar directly into a jar, secure the lid, and shake vigorously until the sugar dissolves. If you're more health conscious, you can use honey, brown sugar, or agave nectar instead. But keep in mind that honey or brown sugar will give the cocktail an amber hue.

Infusing flavor into syrup is just as easy, and you can use almost any fruits, herbs, or spices. Fresh basil, cilantro, mint, and rosemary—as in the Rosemary Lemon Syrup on page 24—are among my favorites. Try infusing syrup with lavender, as in the Lavender Lemon Syrup below. It will transform an average martini into an elegant cocktail. Experiment with spices in syrups, such as cardamom, cinnamon, clove, and curry. Just a tiny amount of syrup made with any of those spices can take the flavor profile of your cocktail to the next level.

You can also substitute herbal tea for water when making simple syrup. I like to use chamomile, jasmine, or orange ginger. They're delicious and convenient if you're in a hurry. Don't be afraid to raid your cabinet and refrigerator and have some fun!

Lavender Lemon Syrup

The fragrance of lavender and lemon add an undeniable sophistication to any cocktail.

2 cups water

¼ cup edible lavender flowers

1½ cups raw sugar or ½ cup agave nectar

3 teaspoons lemon juice

In a medium saucepan, bring the water and lavender to a boil. Add the sugar and stir until it dissolves. Add the lemon juice, reduce the heat, cover, and simmer for 3 to 5 minutes. Remove from the heat and set aside to cool to room temperature. Strain through a fine mesh strainer into a bottle, and refrigerate for up to 1 week. Makes 3 cups.

note: Try it in the Lavender Lemon Tikitini (page 100) or the Lavender Coconut Cocktail (page 118).

Light Simple Syrup

This is a healthier alternative to traditional simple syrups made from refined sugar.

2 cups water

½ cup agave nectar

In a medium saucepan, bring the water to a boil. Whisk in the agave nectar. Remove from the heat and continue whisking until thoroughly blended. Cover and set aside to cool to room temperature. Pour into a bottle, and refrigerate for up to 1 week. Makes 2½ cups.

Use it in the Cucumber Sorbet Saketini (page 161) or the Island Fashioned (page 157).

Rosemary Lemon Syrup

The aroma of fresh rosemary and lemon is extremely calming. It will relax you even before the first sip.

2 cups water

1½ cups raw sugar or ½ cup agave nectar

3 or 4 sprigs fresh rosemary, about 3 inches long

3 teaspoons lemon juice

Add the water and rosemary to a medium saucepan, and bring it to a boil. Stir in the sugar until it dissolves. Add the lemon juice, reduce the heat, cover, and simmer for 3 to 5 minutes. Remove from the heat, and set aside to cool to room temperature. Strain through a fine mesh strainer into a bottle and refrigerate for up to 1 week. Makes 3 cups.

Try this syrup in the Rosemary Lemonade cocktail (page 86).

Purees

To create these purees, you'll need a blender, food processer, or a high-speed blender like NutriBullet™, the last of which is my weapon of choice because it produces a perfectly even and smooth puree in seconds. Use the freshest ingredients available, particularly fruits and vegetables. I shop the Montauk's Farmers Market every summer Thursday for fresh, local produce grown in the area's rich soil. Be sure to rinse all your produce thoroughly first.

As you'll see in the recipes that follow, I add citrus juice, water, or lemonade to give my purees a smooth texture along with a bit of agave nectar to balance the flavors and add some sweetness. When using jalapeño peppers, as in the Hot Basil & Berry Puree (page 27) and the Cucumber, Cilantro & Jalapeño Puree (see below), include the seeds for extra heat if you like more kick. When storing a puree in a plastic squeeze bottle, make sure that the bottle has a mouth large enough for the mixture to flow freely.

Not only will these purees enhance your cocktails, but they're amazing when used in ceviche, added to other seafood dishes, or drizzled on salads. You can puree just about any kind of fruit, vegetable, or fresh herb. Visit your local farmers market for inspiration.

Cucumber, Cilantro & Jalapeño Puree

The beauty of this spicy, cool, refreshing puree lies in its versatility. Use it for a punch of flavor in cocktails, or incorporate it into ceviche or Thai chicken salad and lettuce wraps. Keep a bottle in your fridge, and get creative.

8 medium-size cucumbers

2 to 3 jalapeño peppers

1 large bunch cilantro

2 to 3 ounces Lynn's Lemonade (page 33)

Thoroughly rinse the cucumbers, peppers, and cilantro. Cut the cucumbers in half lengthwise, leaving the skin on for crunch and color. Cut them into 1-inch chunks and set aside.

Cut the jalapeño peppers lengthwise in half. Then slice each half into smaller chunks, up to ¼-inch wide. Leave the seeds for extra heat.

Remove the stems from the cilantro bunch and discard. Lightly chop the cilantro leaves.

Combine the cucumber, jalapeño, and cilantro in a food processor or blender. Add the lemonade and blend until pureed. The mixture should be slightly pulpy. Transfer to a plastic squeeze bottle, and refrigerate for up to 3 days. Makes 3 to 4 cups.

Fennel Orange Puree

This unexpected but delicious blend is perfect during the summer months. Use it in cocktails and on garden salads and fresh seafood.

½ cup fresh chopped fennel

1 medium blood orange, peeled (or 2 Mandarin oranges, peeled)

1 ounce agave nectar

¼ cup water

Combine the fennel, orange, agave nectar, and water in a food processor or blender, and blend until smooth. Transfer to a plastic squeeze bottle, and refrigerate for up to 2 or 3 days. Makes 2 cups.

Hot Basil & Berry Puree

This tropical concoction is great in cocktails, of course, but it's also amazing over lemon sorbet as a delicious dessert.

¾ cup strawberries

½ cup blueberries

8 to 10 large basil leaves

½ jalapeño pepper (use more or less depending on desired heat)

2 ounces agave nectar

2 ounces Lynn's Lemonade (page 33)

Rinse the strawberries, blueberries, basil, and jalapeño thoroughly. Remove the stems from the strawberries and jalapeño. Slice the jalapeño in half lengthwise, leaving the seeds for extra heat. Place in a food processor or blender. Add the agave nectar and lemonade. Blend until smooth. Transfer to a plastic squeeze bottle, and refrigerate for up to 3 days. Makes 2 cups.

Use this in the Hot Basil & Berry Lemonade cocktail (page 64).

Hot Mango Puree

This absolutely excellent puree is delicious in tiki drinks as well as on seafood.

1 jalapeño pepper

2 cups diced mango

½ ounce Sriracha

1½ ounces lime juice

1½ ounces water

1½ ounces agave nectar

Rinse the jalapeño thoroughly and remove the stem. Slice the pepper lengthwise and then across, cutting each piece in half. Place the jalapeño pieces, including the seeds for extra heat, in a food processor or blender. Add the mango, Sriracha, lime juice, water, and agave nectar. Blend until smooth. Transfer to a plastic squeeze bottle, and refrigerate for up to 3 days. Makes 2½ cups.

Add this to the Hot Mango Mamacita, and *ay caramba!*

Mango & Mint Puree

This puree goes into many of my drinks, and it also works well on salads and seafood. You can turn it into a salad dressing by adding fresh lemon juice and olive oil. Don't be afraid to experiment!

2 cups mango chunks

⅔ cup fresh chopped mint

⅛ cup agave nectar

1 ounce Lynn's Lemonade (page 33)

Combine the mango, mint, agave nectar, and lemonade in a food processor or blender and blend until smooth. Transfer to a plastic squeeze bottle, and refrigerate for up to 2 days. Makes 2 cups.

Use this to make the Mango, Mint & Rum Spritzer (page 75).

Smoked Pineapple & Sage Puree

You'll love the surprisingly delicious smoky sweetness of this puree, which can double as a marinade for chicken.

2 cups pineapple chunks

1 ounce agave nectar

¼ cup fresh chopped sage

1 teaspoon smoked hot paprika (adjust to taste)

½ ounce Lynn's Lemonade (page 33)

Combine the pineapple, agave nectar, sage, paprika, and lemonade in a food processor or blender, and blend until smooth. Transfer to a plastic squeeze bottle, and refrigerate up to 2 days. Makes 2½ cups.

Add this to the Mexican Snake Charmer (page 80).

Watermelon & Basil Puree

This fresh and delectable puree offers a sweet, refreshing taste of summer that can be used as a dressing on a fresh tomato and mozzarella salad or on chilled shrimp as an alternative to cocktail sauce. Get creative with it!

1 small seedless watermelon

⅔ cup fresh chopped basil

¼ cup agave nectar

Cut the watermelon in half and scoop out the flesh, taking care not to scoop too close to the bitter rind. Slice the melon into 2-inch cubes and put into blender.

Separate the basil leaves from the stems and tear or chop the leaves into small ½-inch pieces. Add to the watermelon in the food processor or blender. Then add the agave nectar and blend until smooth. Transfer to a plastic squeeze bottle, and refrigerate for up to 3 days. Makes 3 to 4 cups.

This puree adds a hint of fresh herbiness to the Montauk Marine Cooler (page 81).

Infusions

What I love most about infusing liquors is the creativity that it allows. Italians have been infusing and spiking acqua di limone or limonata for generations. Grandmother Fiorita added her fresh limonata and two ice cubes to my grandfather's homemade wine during the hot summer months, garnishing it with fresh basil, thyme, peaches, and plums. She also soaked her home-grown figs and peaches in the red wine that my grandfather made. Pears infused in homemade grappa always made our family gatherings interesting.

To begin, you'll need a 2- to 3-gallon glass jar; these are available in a wide variety of shapes and styles. When using a jar with a spigot, always check for leaks before filling it with a costly, premium liquor. Fill the jar with water, and place a paper towel under the spigot to see if it leaks. Also choose a jar with an airtight lid. Infusion times vary, depending on the ingredients. Pineapples, melons, and berries don't need as much time as dense-skinned cherries. Taste test your creation after a week to check the level of flavor. When using hot peppers, you may want to test it after just 2 or 3 days, at which point you can remove the peppers so your infusion doesn't get too spicy.

Because of its neutral flavor, vodka is the most versatile spirit to infuse. But don't stop there. Bourbons, rums, and tequilas are also delicious when infused with fresh fruits, herbs, spices, and even vegetables such as hot peppers and onions. Gin itself is an infusion, but you can always add to it. The possibilities are endless, so create your own signature infusions with the freshest ingredients for the best results. Then marvel at the bevy of different cocktails that you can make from just one jar and a variety of mixers.

An important note: You may want to sample the fruit as your infusion runs low, but don't. The fruit filters impurities in the liquor and will taste bad. Discard or compost it, and slice some fresh fruit to start a new batch.

Apple Cinnamon Bourbon

This infusion is as American as apple pie. Its smooth apple and cinnamon flavor and aroma are comfort in a jar. You can use it in festive autumn cocktails, serve it warm at holiday celebrations, or pour it over ice with lemonade and fresh mint or fruit during spring or summer. You'll love the versatility of this four-season blend.

10 to 12 Honeycrisp or Gala apples

4 to 6 cinnamon sticks

2 liters Jack Daniel's®, Maker's Mark, or other premium bourbon

Rinse the apples thoroughly and remove the stems. Cut the apples into quarters and place in a large glass jar. Add the cinnamon sticks and bourbon, and close the lid tightly. Let stand on the counter, out of

direct sunlight, for at least 2 weeks, stirring daily. Taste it at the end of the first week and, if you prefer a milder spice profile, remove the cinnamon. Makes approximately 2 liters.

Caribbean Comfort Infusion

Cinnamon is commonly used in many Caribbean cocktails and local cuisine like Jamaican jerk chicken. The essence of cinnamon is said to have a calming effect. Some cultures believe cinnamon is an aphrodisiac. I always connect cinnamon to comfort, which is why I call this infusion Caribbean Comfort.

1 pineapple

2 cinnamon sticks, approximately 4 inches long

1 liter coconut rum

1 liter Bacardi Silver or other light rum

Rinse the pineapple thoroughly, lay it on its side, and slice off the top and bottom. Stand the pineapple upright and cut the skin off the sides in strips, starting at the top. Lay the remaining cylinder of pineapple flesh on its side and cut it into 1- to 2 inch slices. Quarter the slices and place them in a large glass jar. Add the cinnamon sticks and rums, and seal the jar tightly. Let stand on the counter, out of direct sunlight, for at least 1 week. Stir daily. Makes approximately 2 liters.

This blend makes an appearance in the Toasted Coconut (page 133) and the Caribbean Comfort Cocktail (page 124) .

Coco Loco Infusion

This perfectly balanced and versatile infusion is great when chilled and served straight up in a martini glass or on the rocks.

1 pineapple

1¼ liters Milagro® Silver or other premium silver tequila

¾ liter coconut rum

Rinse the pineapple thoroughly, lay it on its side, and slice off the top and bottom. Stand the pineapple upright and cut the skin off the sides in strips, starting at the top. Lay the remaining cylinder of pineapple flesh on its side and cut it into 1- to 2-inch slices. Quarter the slices and place them in a large glass jar. Add the tequila and rum, and seal the jar tightly. Let stand on the counter, out of direct sunlight, for at least 1 week, stirring daily. Makes approximately 2 liters.

This infusion appears in many of the cocktails in this book, including the Brazilian Breezer (page 111) and the Mayan Sunrise (page 77).

Cucumber Chile Pepper Vodka

The coolness of the cucumber in this infusion tames the heat of the pepper and results in a unique, well-balanced flavor.

6 cucumbers

2 Thai chile peppers or 3 to 4 jalapeño peppers

2 liters premium vodka

Rinse the cucumbers and peppers thoroughly. Leaving the skin on, cut the cucumbers into ½-inch slices, and place in a large glass jar. Slice one of the peppers lengthwise to expose the seeds, which will release the heat when placed in the jar. Pour the vodka into the jar and close the lid tightly. Let stand on the counter, out of direct sunlight, for at least 1 week. Stir daily. Makes approximately 2 liters.

Note: Thai chiles sometimes can prove difficult to find and can be too hot for some. Three or four jalapeños would be a good substitute. Several of my signature cocktails use this infusion, including Hot Pink Drink (page 69) and various bloody marys and martinis.

Cucumber Vodka

This is one of the most versatile infusions that you can make. It pairs well with fresh herbs, such as basil, cilantro, and mint, and serves as the base for an extremely smooth and refreshing cocktail each and every time.

4 to 6 large cucumbers

2 liters premium vodka

Rinse the cucumbers thoroughly. Cut off the ends and discard. With a vegetable peeler, remove sections of the skin to create alternating stripes of skin and flesh. Cut the cucumbers into ¼-inch slices and place them into a large glass jar. Add the vodka, secure the lid, and store on the counter, out of direct sunlight, for 1 to 2 weeks. Stir daily. Strain through a fine mesh sieve, then store in the refrigerator in a sealed glass container. Makes approximately 2 liters.

Ginger Lemongrass Vodka

You can also enjoy this infusion on the rocks or chilled and served up in a martini glass.

1 large knob ginger root

8 stalks lemongrass (6 to 8 inches long)

2 liters premium vodka

Using a vegetable peeler, remove the skin from the ginger root. Cut the root into ¼-inch slices, then chop into ¼-inch cubes and place in a large glass jar. Lay the lemongrass stalks on your cutting board and, with a butter knife handle, dent the stalks every inch to release their flavor. Place the stalks in the jar, add the vodka, and close the lid tightly. Let stand on the counter, out of direct sunlight, for at least 10 days, stirring daily. Makes approximately 2 liters.

Note: If your regular grocery store doesn't carry lemongrass or fresh ginger, you can find both in most Asian markets. I use this soothing and delicious blend in my Hukilau Lemonade (page 70).

Lynn's Lemonade

This is a healthy and delicious substitute for sweet and sour mix, traditional powdered lemonades, or juices made from frozen concentrate, all of which are oversweet and loaded with sugar. Agave nectar is a natural sweetener derived from the same plant used to make tequila. In Mexico, the plant is called *aguamiel*, or honey water. The Aztecs believed that it came from the gods, and they used the liquid from its core to flavor foods and drinks. Many health-conscious consumers prefer it as their sweetener of choice.

1 gallon noncarbonated spring water, warmed slightly

½ to 1 cup agave nectar (to taste)

6 lemons

Pour the spring water into a large glass pitcher, making sure to leave enough room for the lemons and nectar. The warmth of the water helps the agave nectar to dissolve thoroughly. You can also place the pitcher in a sunny spot for an hour or so to get the water to the right temperature for blending the ingredients. Add the agave nectar to taste, and stir until it dissolves.

Roll the lemons on a hard surface to release the juice from the fruit pulp. Slice them in half, and strain the juice using a mini strainer or citrus press. Add the juice to the pitcher and stir well. Chill before serving. Makes 1 gallon.

Because it doesn't overpower but subtly complements the other natural flavors in the drinks, you'll find this lemonade in many of my recipes, including April Showers (page 41), Mandarin & Fennel Iced Tea (page 73), and Mexican Snake Charmer (page 80).

Pineapple Jalapeño Vodka

You will find the combination of hot and sweet together is a very pleasant surprise in this infusion, as the pineapple balances the heat wonderfully. In fact, this infusion is amazing just on its own over ice. Feel free to get creative, as there's really no wrong way to enjoy this cocktail.

1 pineapple

4 to 6 large jalapeño peppers

2 liters premium vodka

Rinse the pineapple thoroughly, lay it on its side, and slice off the top and bottom. Stand the pineapple upright and cut the skin off the sides in strips, starting at the top. Lay the remaining cylinder of pineapple flesh on its side and cut it into 1- to 2-inch slices. Quarter the slices and place them in a large glass jar. Slice the peppers in half lengthwise and place them in the jar. Add the vodka and close the lid tightly. Let stand on the counter, out of direct sunlight, for at least 1 week. Stir daily. Makes approximately 2 liters.

This infusion appears in several of my Hula Hut cocktails, including the amazing Mayan Chocolate (page 76).

Pineapple Vanilla Vodka

This infusion soothes and calms the senses and is simply amazing on its own over ice.

1 pineapple

2 to 3 Tahitian vanilla beans (approximately 4 to 6 inches long)

2 liters premium vodka

Rinse the pineapple thoroughly, lay it on its side, and slice off the top and bottom. Stand the pineapple upright and cut the skin off the sides in strips, starting at the top. Lay the remaining cylinder of pineapple flesh on its side and cut it into 1- to 2-inch slices. Quarter the slices and place them in a large glass jar. Score each vanilla bean lengthwise to release the flavor. Place the vanilla beans into the jar, add the vodka, and seal tightly. Let stand on a counter, out of direct sunlight, for at least 1 week, stirring daily. Makes approximately 2 liters.

This sweet and earthy infusion goes into many of my cocktails, such as the Tahitian Lemon Drop (page 103) and Mellow Yellow (page 78).

Pink Lemonade

Pomegranates are an exception to my juicing rule. Separating the seeds from the rind and then the juice from the seeds should qualify as an Olympic event. Better to buy pomegranate juice, but make sure that it's 100 percent pure pomegranate juice. I like the Pom® brand, which most grocery stores carry.

1 gallon noncarbonated warm
   spring water

1 cup unsweetened pomegranate juice

½ to 1 cup agave nectar (to taste)

6 fresh lemons

Pour the spring water into a large glass pitcher, making sure to leave enough room for the other ingredients. The water should be slightly warm. The warm water helps the agave nectar dissolve thoroughly. You can also place the pitcher of water in a sunny spot for an hour or so to get the water to the right temperature for blending the ingredients. Add the pomegranate juice and agave nectar to taste, and stir until the nectar dissolves.

Roll the lemons on a hard surface to release the juice from the fruit pulp. Slice them in half and strain the juice using a mini strainer or citrus press. Add the juice and stir well. Chill before serving. Makes about 1 gallon.

Tahitian Blend Infusion

I use this blend year round in practically everything, especially eggnog and warm cider during the holidays.

1 knob ginger root (about 4 inches)

2 liters aged rum

3 Tahitian vanilla beans, split lengthwise

4 cloves

2 or 3 cinnamon sticks (about 4 inches
   long)

½ teaspoon freshly grated nutmeg

zest of 1 Mandarin orange (avoid the
   bitter pith)

2 Honeycrisp apples

Peel the ginger root, cut it into ⅛-inch slices, and place the slices in the bottom of a large glass jar. Add the rum, vanilla beans, cloves, cinnamon sticks, nutmeg, orange zest, and apples. Secure the lid, and store on the counter, out of direct sunlight, for 1 to 2 weeks before serving. Makes approximately 2 liters.

Techniques

Before you begin, have all of your tools at hand and ingredients prepared ahead of time. A good rule of thumb: always smile, and never let 'em see you sweat! I prepare pitchers of cocktails ahead of time and store them in the refrigerator for up to 2 days before serving. Batching drinks—the industry term—allows you to get more creative, but remember to write down measurements and ingredients as you go. Trust me, you won't remember if you taste test along the way . . . and you must straw-taste your creations before you serve them.

BLEND

When using an immersion blender, keep the blades well below the surface of the liquid. You don't want to wind up wearing your cocktail. When making frozen drinks, pulse in short bursts to break up the ice without breaking the motor.

CHILL

If you don't have time to chill your martini glasses thoroughly in the freezer before making your drink, fill the glasses with icewater while you make the drink.

MUDDLE

When muddling herbs and other flora, press firmly to extract the plants' essences and oils—but don't mash them. Press harder to crush fruit.

RIM

When rimming a cocktail glass, start by squeezing the garnish or one of the garnishes (lemon, lime, jalapeño, or pineapple for example) around the outside edge of the glass; then roll the outside edge in the salt, sugar, or other rimming mixture. That way the mixture won't blend into the drink and change the way it's supposed to taste.

SHAKE

Do it like bartenders do: horizontally over the shoulder. But make sure the cap's on tight. You want to shake your drink—not hurl it behind you!

HULA HUT

COCKTAILS

MY PASSION FOR EXOTIC COCKTAILS EMERGED WHEN A FRIEND AND I RODE a motorcycle around the Mayan Riviera of Mexico, from Merida to Belize. It was still rural then, with few stops other than the occasional tiki bar on a remote beach. The drinks were simple and had few ingredients—just fresh fruits and juices mixed with tequila or rum. But they were absolutely delicious and much more refreshing than the sugary concoctions served stateside. Call it love in a coconut cup. That experience and many like it changed the way I make drinks, providing the inspiration for what are now my signature cocktails at Lynn's Hula Hut.

Many of these cocktails intentionally consist of ingredients that I can source locally. Whether in Montauk or abroad, I always search for the nearest farm stand or fruit tree. There's nothing better than stumbling upon those small, out-of-the-way places to eat and drink and venturing through an overgrown tropical path to find sugar-white sand caressed by a translucent, aquamarine sea. These cocktails will help you capture the feeling of that same experience wherever you may be.

April Showers

Lemon verbena is prized for its intoxicating citrus aroma. This drink's winning combination of bracing cucumber, sweet elderflower liqueur, and the scent of lemon verbena provides a calming sensation from the first sip. It's as refreshing as warm sunshine after a cool spring shower.

3 cucumber slices,
plus 1 for garnish

½ ounce St-Germain® or
other elderflower liqueur

1½ ounces Cucumber
Vodka (page 32)

Lynn's Lemonade (page 33)

1 sprig lemon verbena
for garnish

Place the cucumber slices in the bottom of a Collins glass, add the elderflower liqueur, and muddle. Fill the glass with ice and add the vodka. Top with lemonade, then pour the contents of the glass into a cocktail shaker. Shake vigorously for 5 seconds. Return the cocktail to the glass, garnish with the lemon verbena sprig and the remaining cucumber slice, and serve with a straw.

Blue Bayou Lemonade

Louisiana is a melting pot of Spanish, West African, French, Native American, and Caribbean cultures. French Caribbean culture made a significant mark on New Orleans because half of the population in the early 1800s arrived from Haiti after the mass exodus following the Haitian Revolution. As a result, Creole culture and Voodoo made an indelible mark on Louisiana. Many more emigrants from St. Barts and St. Maarten settled in Louisiana, establishing a colorful community while incorporating additional aspects of Caribbean architecture, food, and music into Louisiana's culture. Cajun and Caribbean colonies also sprang up along the many bayous where fish, game, and fruits were plentiful. This cocktail is a staple at my friend Luke's fishing camps in southwestern Louisiana.

¼ cup blueberries

½ ounce agave nectar

2½ ounces premium bourbon

6 ounces Lynn's Lemonade (page 33)

1 lemon wheel (page 15) for garnish

Rinse the berries thoroughly and place them in the bottom of a 12-ounce mason jar. Add the agave nectar and muddle well. Add the bourbon, fill the jar with ice, and top with the lemonade. Garnish with the lemon wheel, and enjoy, y'all!

note: You can substitute wild berries found along the bayous in Louisiana for the blueberries.

Boudreaux's Bayou Berry Tea

My wild and crazy Cajun buddy Boudreaux kidnapped me and a friend from the Maple Leaf Bar in the Leonidas neighborhood of New Orleans many moons ago. He drove us to the swamp for a *fais do-do*—a Cajun dance celebration—at his brother's fishing camp. For three fun-filled days and nights, we feasted on alligator boudin, crawfish, and muscadine moonshine. This is my version of Boudreaux's hard-hitting berry moonshine, smooth but not quite as hard.

4 muscadine berries, plus extra for garnish

juice of half a lemon

2½ ounces Maker's Mark or other premium bourbon

1 ounce agave nectar

sassafras tea

1 sugarcane stalk for garnish

1 satsuma section for garnish

Cut the berries in half and muddle them with the lemon juice in a pint-sized mason jar. Add the bourbon and agave nectar, and fill the jar with ice. Add the tea to within 1 or 2 inches from the top. Secure the lid on the jar and shake for a few seconds. Remove the lid and stir the drink with the sugarcane stalk, leaving it in for presentation. Garnish with additional berries and a satsuma section.

note: *Muscadine berries are large, dark purple berries about the size of a grape. They grow wild in southern Louisiana near the bayous and teem with antioxidants. If you don't live in the Pelican State, you can make the following substitutions: blackberries for muscadine, black or green tea for the sassafras, a straw for the sugarcane stalk, and a garden-variety orange for the satsuma.*

Bourbon Bash

Names have been withheld to protect the not so innocent, but the Boys on the Bus, as I call them, inspired this cocktail. A few years ago, a bunch of southern guys drove up from the Carolinas for their annual trip to participate in one of several fishing tournaments held in Montauk Harbor. Their touring bus dropped anchor for several days in a parking lot near the Hula Hut, which hadn't opened yet. They sat and watched as I shoveled sand, planted palms, and readied the bar for the season. Introducing themselves, they said, "You need a break. Try this." I took a swig from the mason jar they handed me. Deliciously smooth. I chugged some more, and one of them said, "Whoa, simmer down now, girl. That's moonshine." Before long, their lightning in a bottle sent me to my hammock for a nice, long nap, but it also prompted this delicious drink. Thanks, guys!

2½ ounces Apple Cinnamon Bourbon (page 29)

1 ounce passion fruit nectar

Lynn's Lemonade (page 33)

1 star fruit for garnish

Fill a pilsner or Collins glass with crushed ice. Add the bourbon and passion fruit nectar, and top with lemonade. Transfer to a cocktail shaker, shake for a few seconds, and return the drink to the glass. Slice a star fruit into ¼-inch sections, and on one of them make a small cut between two of the points. Pierce the fruit slice with a paper parasol, place the fruit on the rim of the glass, and serve with a straw. (See the table of contents page for the drink without the parasol or straw.)

Coconut Cucumber Mojito

This cocktail is one of the most popular mojitos at the Hula Hut. Cool, refreshing cucumber sourced locally and fresh mint grown onsite make it delicious and dangerously smooth. Sip it slowly, and savor the flavor.

5 mint leaves

3 lime wheels (page 15)

3 cucumber wheels (page 15)

½ ounce agave nectar

2 ounces coconut rum

club soda, chilled

1 sprig mint for garnish

1 (4-inch) sugarcane stalk for garnish

Place the mint, lime, cucumber, and agave nectar in a large rocks glass. Muddle gently. Fill the glass with crushed ice and add the coconut rum. Transfer the contents to a cocktail shaker and shake for a few seconds. Pour the cocktail back into the glass and top with a splash of club soda. Garnish with a mint sprig, sugarcane stalk, and an optional cucumber wheel.

SUGARCANE

A kind of tropical grass, sugarcane is the world's largest production crop. Some 80 percent of commercial sugar comes from sugarcane, which is harvested in more than 90 countries today, primarily Brazil. Portuguese settlers first planted it there in the early 1500s, establishing the first large-scale production of the crop. Over the course of the sixteenth century, the demand and price for sugarcane skyrocketed because sugar had replaced honey as the preferred sweetener for European recipes, particularly jams and jellies. By the middle of the seventeenth century, mills popped up throughout Brazil as the country established itself as the world's premier sugarcane producer. But that success met with competition, especially from the Caribbean, where various islands sought a piece of the lucrative sugar trade. Sugarcane ultimately helped shaped expansion, colonization, and control of the New World and remains a staple in the tropics as well as in the glass of a tropical drink. It also still grows in abundance in southern Louisiana. Stalks of raw sugarcane, used in some tiki cocktails, add a layer of enjoyment because you can chew the stalks to extract the sweet juice.

Fortaleza Kiwi Caipirinha

Many years ago, my friend Marco rented a place on the northeast coast of Brazil in Fortaleza, the windsurfing and kite surfing capital of the world, where spectacular dunes cascade onto a white sandy beach. Our daily menu often consisted of freshly caught fish purchased from local fishermen along with an abundance of coconuts, kiwis, limes, and of course cachaça, the Brazilian liquor made from fresh sugarcane juice—a real bargain then and there at just a couple of dollars per liter. Brazil's national cocktail, the Caipirinha, makes good use of cachaça, and I recreated the drink with a sweet and sexy kiwi twist. Kiwi fruit contains more vitamin C than oranges and has a wonderful tangy sweetness. Sip a Fortaleza Kiwi Caipirinha while watching the sun sink into the sea.

half a kiwi fruit

1 lime

2 tablespoons granulated sugar

2½ ounces cachaça

1 lime wheel for garnish

Using a vegetable peeler or paring knife, remove the skin from the kiwi fruit. Cut the kiwi into small chunks and place in a rocks glass. Roll the lime on a hard surface to release the juices, and cut into eight wedges. Place the lime wedges in the glass, add the sugar, and muddle well. Add some crushed ice and the cachaça, and shake vigorously. Use your hips, and serve with a wink. Garnish with a lime wheel.

note: If your local liquor store doesn't carry cachaça, use an aged Jamaican rum. I prefer Appleton® Estate aged rum.

Gin Beach Breeze

Gin Beach lies beyond Montauk's jetty, surrounded by water, where few tourists venture. The peaceful beauty of this secluded spot is unmatched, and a chilled pitcher of this delicious cocktail is like the refreshing ocean breeze there in liquid form.

8 ounces premium dry gin

8 ounces pomegranate juice

6 ounces grapefruit juice

2 ounces lime juice

1 ounce pineapple juice

4 lime wedges (page 15) for garnish

Combine the gin and juices in a large container or pitcher, approximately 32 ounces. Secure with a lid and lightly shake. Refrigerate for up to 3 days or, better yet, put the container in a cooler packed with ice and head to the beach!

Fill four highball glasses with ice, shake the mixture lightly again, and pour evenly into each of the glasses. Garnish each with a lime wedge and enjoy.

SERVES 4

Gin Bellini

This drink is an excellent choice for a sophisticated summer brunch and pairs perfectly with oysters, fresh fruits, and light crêpes. Giuseppe Cipriani concocted this sparkling wine cocktail in the early 1900s while tending bar in Venice, Italy, and he named it after Italian Renaissance painter Giovanni Bellini. The original calls specifically for Prosecco, although some establishments prefer to use Champagne or Champagne-style sparkling wines. You can use either. As with a mimosa, I prefer to add the sweet tropical flavors of mango and agave nectar. For an added twist, this recipe uses a garnish of thyme instead of the standard cherry or strawberry. However you make it, always serve this refreshing cocktail cold.

1 ounce Boodles® or other premium dry gin

¼ ounce Campari®

¼ ounce mango nectar

1 teaspoon agave nectar or light brown sugar

Prosecco or dry sparkling wine

1 sprig thyme for garnish

In a cocktail shaker, combine the gin, Campari, mango nectar, and agave nectar with ice. Shake for about 10 seconds, then strain into a chilled champagne flute. Top with your favorite sparkling wine and garnish with the thyme sprig.

Great White Bite

The waters off Montauk teem with a variety of sharks, including the blue, mako, thresher, and infamous great white. On August 6, 1986, legendary Montauk shark fisherman Frank Mundus landed the world's largest great white shark aboard the *Cricket II*. The shark tipped the scales at 3,427 pounds! Before the Hula Hut opened, my friend Carl asked me to set up my traveling tiki bar on the dock at his marina during one of the local shark tournaments. I wanted to create a new twist on the traditional margarita, and it had to have a bite—a great white bite! Another friend, David—a local farmer known as the "Pepper Guru"—sold me some jalapeño peppers and fresh cilantro, and off I went. After some experimenting, the Great White Bite took shape. The next day, I pulled into the marina and served up the concoction, and the Great White Bite became an instant hit. Locals call it the Shark Bite Margarita, and it's still a top seller at the Hula Hut.

1 lime

2 ounces Patrón® or other silver tequila

¾ ounce Cointreau®

1 teaspoon Cucumber, Cilantro & Jalapeño Puree (page 25)

Lynn's Lemonade (page 33)

kosher salt for rimming

1 sprig cilantro for garnish

Slice the lime in half and squeeze the juice from one of the halves into a cocktail shaker filled with ice. Add the tequila, Cointreau, and puree. Top with lemonade and shake for about 10 seconds while dancing to salsa music. Rim a margarita or rocks glass with lime and salt, then strain the mixture into the glass. Garnish with a cilantro sprig or a lime wedge made from the other half of the lime.

Guava Mint Caipirinha

The guava, a pear-shaped, greenish-yellow tropical fruit, grows in Mexico, South America, and parts of Asia. This sweet and delicious fruit is loaded with vitamin C and fiber. It's good for your skin, it helps lower blood pressure, and because it's high in fiber and lower in sugar than most tropical fruits, it's great for weight loss. It's also delicious when paired with mint and cachaça, as you'll see when you try this cocktail.

3 or 4 fresh mint leaves

3 lime slices, about ⅛-inch thick

¼ ounce agave nectar or ½ tablespoon brown sugar

2 ounces cachaça

1½ ounces guava nectar

1 sprig mint for garnish

Place the mint leaves in the bottom of a cocktail shaker. Cover them with the lime slices and gently muddle. Add the agave nectar, cachaça, and guava nectar. Add ice and shake for about 15 seconds. Strain into a rocks glass filled with ice and garnish with the mint sprig.

tiki tip: For best results, play some smooth Brazilian jazz in the background while you make this drink.

Hanalei Bay Breeze

Hanalei Bay sits on the north shore of Kaua'i, the oldest of the Hawaiian Islands. It's known as the Garden Isle, and it's one of the most magical places on Earth. This drink will take you there.

2 ounces coconut rum

1 ounce premium light rum

1 ounce premium spiced rum

4 ounces pineapple juice

4 ounces pomegranate juice

1 ounce lime juice

1 ounce premium dark rum, divided in halves

2 Traverse City Cherry Bombs (page 14)

2 pineapple wedges (page 20)

In a large cocktail shaker, combine the coconut, light, and spiced rums with the pineapple, pomegranate, and lime juices. Add ice and shake for about 10 seconds. Fill two Collins glasses with ice and strain the cocktail evenly into each glass. Float ½ ounce of dark rum atop each cocktail, and top each with a cherry. Spear either the cherries or the pineapple wedges with a paper parasol, rest it on the edge of glass, and serve.

SERVES 2

TRAVERSE CITY CHERRIES

At the base of Lake Michigan's Grand Traverse Bay lies Traverse City, Michigan. About 20 miles west you'll find Sleeping Bear Dunes National Lakeshore, a natural formation with miles of sandy beaches and "perched dunes" created by glaciers towering 450 feet above Lake Michigan's northwest coast. This part of Michigan's Lower Peninsula is not only a beautiful spot for outdoor recreation in both summer and winter—among its beautiful beaches, picturesque peninsulas, and surrounding countryside—but its relatively mild climate and fertile soils make it perfect for growing many varieties of fruit. Traverse City is known as the Cherry Capital of the World, with more than 4 million tart cherry trees that produce 75 percent of the tart cherries grown in America. In a state with more freshwater coastline than any other—where you're never more than 6 miles from water—boaters stock their coolers with tiki drinks all summer long. Even on the Great Lakes, tiki culture is alive and well!

Hibiscus Lemonade

In the late fifteenth century, Christopher Columbus came upon the Virgin Islands, naming them after the legend of St. Ursula and her 11,000 virgin followers, and the crowns of half of Europe wrestled for control of them. The Danish West India Company established the first permanent settlement on St. Thomas in 1672, and soon after plantations sprung up around the islands, growing sugar cane, cotton, and indigo. In the late seventeenth century, the English gained control of Tortola, Anegada, and Virgin Gorda. These three eastern islands and around 60 smaller ones surrounding them today comprise the British Virgin Islands. After World War I, the United States recognized the region's strategic location and purchased St. John, St. Thomas, and St. Croix from Denmark. In 1969, the trade embargo against Cuba prompted many travelers seeking tropical sun, white sand, and warm waters to turn to the Virgin Islands, making them a popular destination. A winter I spent there years ago inspired the creation of this cocktail. Keep a large jar of it in the fridge to cool you off on a hot tropical day.

½ cup boiling water

1 hibiscus tea bag

1 tablespoon raw honey

2 ounces Ginger Lemongrass Vodka (page 32)

2 ounces Lynn's Lemonade (page 33)

⅛ teaspoon fresh ginger, minced

1 edible orchid or hibiscus flower (page 17) for garnish

Pour the water into a large cup or mug and add the tea bag and honey. Let steep for several minutes. Cool to room temperature and refrigerate for up to 3 days before serving.

In a cocktail shaker, add the chilled hibiscus tea, vodka, lemonade, and ginger. Shake with ice for about 10 seconds. Strain into a medium mason jar or pint glass filled with ice. Garnish with an edible orchid and serve with a straw.

Hot Basil & Berry Lemonade

This cocktail will take your mouth on a flavorful joyride. It's everything I love in one glass and perfect on a hot summer afternoon. Some say that it's the heat of this drink that cools you off. You'll have to try one or two to find out for sure.

1½ ounces Tito's vodka

¼ ounce Green Chartreuse

2½ ounces Hot Basil & Berry Puree (page 27)

Lynn's Lemonade (page 33)

1 large blackberry for garnish

1 sprig basil for garnish

Fill a pint glass with ice. Add the vodka, Chartreuse, and puree, and top with the lemonade. Transfer to a cocktail shaker, shake, and return to the glass. Repeat. (Yep, do it twice. You're aerating, chilling, and diluting the drink to its proper serving point.)

Garnish with the blackberry, basil sprig, and an optional jalapeño pepper slice.

Hot Mango Mamacita

Holy mother of mango, this is one spicy cocktail! The secret is the Hot Mango Puree, which contains jalapeño and Sriracha, the popular hot sauce made from chile peppers, vinegar, garlic, sugar, and salt. Add more or less depending on your comfort level. The cool crispness of the lime juice, lemonade, and ice will help balance the heat.

2 ounces Patrón or other premium silver tequila

½ ounce Cointreau

¼ ounce lime juice

3 ounces Hot Mango Puree (page 27)

kosher salt for rimming (optional)

Lynn's Lemonade (page 33)

lime wedge (page 15) for garnish

Fill a pint glass with ice. Add the tequila, Cointreau, lime juice, and puree. Transfer to a shaker and shake for about 5 seconds. Salt the rim of the glass if you like. Return the drink to the glass and top with the lemonade. Garnish with a lime wedge or twist. For that extra wow, add a jalapeño slice and edible orchid.

Hot Pineapple Sake Spritzer

You won't find sake in tiki drinks often, but sake did appear in Polynesian and then tiki culture around World War II when a number of the Pacific islands supported American military bases against Japan. Japanese fighter pilots, known as kamikazes—from the Japanese words for "divine wind" and for which the popular kamikaze drink is named—drank sake prior to carrying out their missions. This cold cocktail is refreshing and smooth—but don't be fooled. This one might just knock your sake off!

1 ounce Pineapple Jalapeño Vodka (page 34)

splash of pineapple juice

1 ounce dry sake

club soda, chilled

1 pineapple wedge (page 20) for garnish

Fill a Collins glass with crushed ice. Add the vodka and the pineapple juice. Add the sake and top with club soda. Garnish with a pineapple wedge and serve with a straw.

Hot Pink Drink

The refreshing sensation of cucumber and the heat of the chiles tastefully balance with the cool, fresh mint. This cocktail will definitely take your taste buds on an interesting ride to Thailand's part of the Pacific Rim. Take a sip, close your eyes, and feel the warm breezes of Phuket. This great summer drink will pleasantly surprise your guests.

2½ ounces Cucumber Chile Pepper Vodka (page 32)

5 ounces Pink Lemonade (page 35)

2 or 3 spearmint or mint leaves

1 lemon wheel (page 15) for garnish

1 sprig spearmint or mint for garnish

Fill a highball glass with ice and add the vodka and pink lemonade. Tear the spearmint leaves to release their flavor and add them to the drink. (Don't muddle them.) Stir with a straw and garnish with a lemon wheel or a mint sprig as shown on the table of contents page.

note: This cocktail is dedicated to Tracy and Joy, both breast cancer survivors and two of my dearest friends. It's also dedicated to those who lost the battle and to the brave women around the world who continue the fight.

Hukilau Lemonade

Hukilau is an ancient Hawaiian form of fishing using a cast net. Several fishermen drag the net along the shore in waist-deep water while family and friends gather on the beach to sing traditional *hukilau* songs to inspire the fishermen and celebrate the catch. A modern day *hukilau* celebration takes place every year in Fort Lauderdale, Florida. Thousands of fun-loving partygoers gather in Polynesian style—flowered shirts, coconut bras, leis, and even ukuleles in tow. Coconuts filled with Polynesian concoctions and decorated with drink umbrellas abound as the music of Martin Denny and Dick Dale fills the warm air. Put it on your bucket list, and make a bucket of this cocktail to share when you're there.

2½ ounces Ginger Lemongrass Vodka (page 32)

1 small scoop of lemon sorbet, about ⅓ cup

Lynn's Lemonade (page 33)

1 lemon wheel (page 15) for garnish

brown sugar for garnish

1 sprig thyme for garnish

Fill a large brandy snifter with crushed ice. Add the vodka and sorbet, and top with the lemonade. Coat the lemon wheel in brown sugar. Garnish the drink with the lemon wheel along with a sprig of fresh thyme. Then lie back in a hammock and celebrate catching some rays.

Lotta Colada

The classic Puerto Rican Piña Colada inspired this cocktail, and it's a huge hit at the Hula Hut. This version of the drink is shaken, and you can't have just one.

1½ ounces premium silver rum

½ ounce dark crème de cacao

½ ounce Frangelico® or other hazelnut liqueur

2 ounces Coco López® cream of coconut

2½ ounces pineapple juice

1 Drunken Pineapple Wedge (page 21) for garnish

1 Traverse City Cherry Bomb (page 14) for garnish

In a small hurricane glass (approximately 12 ounces), combine the rum, crème de cacao, hazelnut liqueur, cream of coconut, and pineapple juice. Fill to the top with crushed ice. Transfer to a cocktail shaker and shake for about 3 seconds. Return the mixture to the glass. Garnish with the pineapple wedge, drop in the cherry, and serve with a straw.

note: You can also blend this cocktail and serve it frozen. Instead of shaking it, transfer the ingredients to a blender and blend for approximately 20 seconds, until smooth. Garnish and serve as above.

Mandarin & Fennel Iced Tea

Cultivated in the Mediterranean, fennel appears widely in Italian and Greek cuisine. The herb has an anise-like flavor but is sweeter and more aromatic. Fennel is said to promote bone health and prevent heart disease, and it has been used in the preparation of absinthe since the late eighteenth century. (Absinthe originally was served as a medicinal elixir.) Fennel also helps create an extremely crisp and refreshing combination when paired with Mandarin orange and lemon, as you'll taste in this delicious summertime drink.

½ cup boiling water

1 Mandarin orange tea bag

1 tablespoon raw honey

1½ ounces dry gin

1 ounce Lynn's Lemonade (page 33)

2 ounces Fennel Orange Puree (page 27)

1 orange wheel (page 15) for garnish

1 sprig fennel for garnish

Pour the water into a large cup or mug, and add the tea bag and honey. Let steep for several minutes. Cool to room temperature. This can be refrigerated up to three days.

Fill a medium-sized mason jar (approximately 12 ounces) with ice. Add the chilled tea, gin, lemonade, and puree. Stir, then garnish with an orange wheel and the fennel.

Mango, Mint & Rum Spritzer

This cocktail is refreshingly simple and easy on the waistline, but I bet you didn't know that mangos are said to prevent cancer, lower cholesterol, fight acne, and even increase your sex drive. This delicious fruit is loaded with vitamins A and E, which are crucial to maintaining eyesight and a healthy alkaline balance. The fresh mint, grown on site at Lynn's Hula Hut, aids in digestion and beautifully balances the rum and mango. Let's toast to your health!

2 ounces Appleton Estate™ or other golden rum

2 ounces Mango & Mint Puree (page 28)

1 or 2 dashes bitters

club soda, chilled

1 lime wheel (page 15) for garnish

1 sprig mint for garnish

Fill a Collins glass with ice. Add the rum, puree, and bitters, then top with club soda. Garnish with a lime wheel or twist, mint sprig, and an optional mango spear, and serve with a straw.

Mayan Chocolate

Montauk juts out into the warm Atlantic Ocean, but it still lies just 20 miles from Connecticut, meaning that it experiences those long and brutal New England winters. One winter, to escape the cold I headed down to the Mayan Riviera, hardly an exclusive resort spot at the time. It still had dirt roads, dense jungle, and the occasional watering hole with swings instead of bar stools. On a blissfully hot day, I happened upon a tiny Mayan family's grilled chicken stand. Jorge grilled up the most amazing split chickens while his wife, Maria, and their four children plucked the animals for the next meal. After the most succulent dish of grilled chicken made with a red pepper dry rub, rice, beans, and pico de gallo, I fell in love. To show my appreciation, I made a donation at an altar dedicated to Our Lady of Fátima, ceremoniously surrounded by candles bearing the image of Jesus. To show the family's gratitude in return, Maria's grandmother gave me the most amazing gift: homemade Mexican chocolate. This delicacy—crafted long before artisanal chocolate makers copied the idea—changed the way I look at cooking. That unexpected sensation of sweet and spicy tasted of pure genius. This is my version of that game-changing Mayan chocolate bar.

3 ounces Pineapple Jalapeño Vodka (page 34)

1 ounce dark crème de cacao

1 pineapple wedge (page 20) for garnish

dark chocolate syrup for garnish

Add the vodka and crème de cacao to a cocktail shaker, and dry shake (no ice) for a few seconds. Pour into an ice-filled rocks glass. Dip only the point of the pineapple wedge in chocolate syrup. Then pierce the wedge with a bamboo skewer and lay it across the top of the glass.

note: You can also serve this cocktail as a dessert martini. To do so, rub the edge of a martini glass with a slice of jalapeño pepper and rim with brown sugar. Serve straight up.

Mayan Sunrise

In the 1990s, Mexico's Mayan Coast was still very rural. Few Americans had discovered its charms. Then mostly Brazilians, Italians, and Spaniards ventured to explore that corner of the Yucatán. But a friend and I motorbiked down the coast to Belize without a care in the world. Every so often, we hung a sharp left to find a secluded beach where we cooled off in the sparkling waters of the Caribbean. To our delight, we discovered a few amazing casitas on the beach that served tequila and fresh *sandia* (watermelon juice). Drinks made there with fresh pineapples, coconut, and mangos changed the way I looked at cocktails. One of my favorite memories from that trip is sitting on the beach in Tulum and watching the sun rise over the water. The beauty of that spiritual experience served as my inspiration for this cocktail.

9 ounces Coco Loco Infusion (page 31)

7 ounces pineapple juice

7 ounces pomegranate juice

2 ounces lime juice

4 dashes grenadine

4 pineapple wedges (page 20) for garnish

4 Traverse City Cherry Bombs (page 14) for garnish

Pour the Coco Loco Infusion and juices into a large glass pitcher. Stir and chill.

Fill four large rocks glasses with crushed ice. Stir the chilled mixture again, then pour evenly into each glass. Add a dash of grenadine to each cocktail and garnish with a pineapple wedge and rum-soaked cherry.

Because you should never watch the sunrise alone, this recipe serves 4.

note: You also can batch this drink by making it in a large jar with a lid. Prepare it the same way, but shake it instead of stirring, and refrigerate for up to 3 days.

Mellow Yellow

This cocktail evokes the tropical climes of Jamaica, where I experienced ginger beer for the first time at a little beach shack in Negril. The sweetness of the pineapple nicely crowns the interplay of the spicy ginger and the smooth vanilla.

2 ounces Pineapple Vanilla Vodka (page 34)

1 ounce pineapple juice

1 teaspoon lime juice

ginger beer

1 pineapple wedge (page 20) for garnish

1 vanilla pod for garnish

To a highball glass filled with ice, add the vodka, pineapple juice, and lime juice, then top with ginger beer to the rim. Garnish with a pineapple wedge and the vanilla pod.

note: *Jamaica's spices and fruits have influenced many tiki drinks over the years. Cucumber juice, ginger beer, lime and mango juices, and pineapple soda all come from Jamaica, and all will elevate your tiki cocktails to deliciously new levels. Jamaica is also renowned for its rums, including Appleton Estate, the oldest sugar estate and distillery on the island. For more than 265 years, Appleton has been crafting world-class rums that continue to find their way into a variety of cocktails, from Jamaica's own Planter's Punch to classic tiki drinks like the Zombie (page 168).*

Mexican Snake Charmer

First created by monks in the South of France, Green Chartreuse is a sweet and spicy liqueur originally used for medicinal purposes in the 1700s. It reportedly makes use of 130 different herbs, flowers, and other secret ingredients, which help this cocktail take you on a magic carpet ride. Just a small amount can create a unique flavor, especially when paired with smoked paprika and pineapple.

2 ounces Patrón or other premium silver tequila

¼ ounce Green Chartreuse

3½ ounces Smoked Pineapple & Sage Puree (page 28)

1½ ounces Lynn's Lemonade (page 33)

2 or 3 dashes Texas Pete® or other hot sauce

1 lime wedge (page 15) for garnish

1 sprig sage for garnish

Fill a large rocks glass (approximately 12 ounces) with ice. Add the tequila, Chartreuse, puree, lemonade, and hot sauce. Transfer to a cocktail shaker and shake for about 5 seconds. Return the mixture to the glass and garnish with a lime wedge and the sage.

note: *If you can't make the puree before you make this mesmerizing cocktail, use the following ingredients as a substitution: 3 ounces pineapple juice, ¼ ounce lime juice, and ⅛ teaspoon smoked paprika. Also, every hot sauce is different. It's fine to use another brand that you prefer. I like Texas Pete because of its bold pepper flavor with the warmth of cayenne.*

Montauk Marine Cooler

A wild group of women on a bachelorette party bar crawl, sporting sexy sailor outfits and phallic party favors, wandered into Lynn's Hula Hut one sunny afternoon. Some of the local fishermen are out at sea for weeks at a time, so this could have been a dangerous situation, but the women held their own, and everyone had a great time. As we say, "What happens at Lynn's Hula Hut *never* stays at Lynn's Hula Hut!" Later the girls asked me to create a refreshing cocktail for them. Its name nodding to their outfits, this drink encompasses everything summertime: the deep blue of the sea, fresh grown watermelon, and the aroma of the basil that reminds me of the sweet smell of privet, which grows in abundance on the East End. I swear like a sailor that you'll love this cooler!

1¼ ounces Patrón or other silver tequila

1¼ ounces Tito's vodka

¼ ounce blue curaçao

Lynn's Lemonade (page 33)

Watermelon & Basil Puree (page 28)

1 watermelon wedge (page 19) for garnish

1 fresh basil leaf for garnish

Fill a Collins or large martini glass with ice, and add the tequila, vodka, and blue curaçao. Add the lemonade to fill the glass three-quarters full. Transfer to a cocktail shaker, and shake for a few seconds. Return the mixture to the glass, and top with the puree. Garnish with an orange wheel, as on the table of contents page, or a watermelon wedge and a fresh basil leaf on a bamboo skewer.

Nutty Samoan

In Denver, my girlfriends and I went to Aspen for the annual Ruggerfest (or the Eye Candy Fest, as we fondly called it). This annual rugby tournament draws thousands of spectators and partygoers to watch teams annihilate one another and then drink and sing tribal songs. Many of the players come from Tonga, Fiji, and Samoa, where rugby remains a hugely popular sport. This drink is dedicated to the fond memory of Ben Masoe and the boys performing the *haka* in their underwear at 3:00 a.m.

2 ounces coconut rum

½ ounce Frangelico or other hazelnut liqueur

3 ounces orange juice

3 ounces pomegranate juice

1 squeeze lime juice

1 orange wheel (page 15) for garnish

1 edible orchid (page 17) for garnish

Fill a Collins glass with ice. Add the rum, hazelnut liqueur, orange juice, pomegranate juice, and lime juice. Transfer to a cocktail shaker and shake for a few seconds. Return the mixture to the glass and garnish with the orange wheel, orchid, and an optional lime twist.

note: The haka is a traditional, ancestral war dance performed to intimidate enemies or opponents. The dance was originally carried out by warriors before battle. They would stomp their feet and scream and shout to announce their power and strength. But this colorful dance with its celebrated war cry is also used to welcome important guests or to pay homage to a significant event, like a funeral.

Papaya Bourbon Cider

Papaya is a must-have for tiki cocktails. This soft, buttery tropical fruit, which originated in Mexico and spread throughout the Caribbean, provides plenty of sweetness along with a wonderful orange hue. Columbus prized the fruit when he sailed the globe. Papayas are rich in vitamin C and fiber, and they contain enzymes that may help treat allergies and injuries. You can enjoy this cocktail all year long. This is the warm-weather version, but you can serve it with warm cider during the holidays.

2 ounces Apple Cinnamon Bourbon (page 29)

3 ounces papaya nectar

¼ ounce agave nectar

1 ounce fresh lemon juice

2 to 3 ounces chilled apple cider

1 lemon wheel (page 15) for garnish

1 cinnamon stick for garnish

Fill a medium-sized mason jar (approximately 12 ounces) with ice. Add the bourbon infusion, papaya nectar, agave nectar, and lemon juice. Top with the apple cider and tumble into a cocktail shaker. Shake for about 3 seconds. Return the mixture to the mason jar and garnish with a lemon wheel and cinnamon stick. Serve with a straw.

Rosemary Lemonade

Lois, the dearest gin snob I've known, proudly claims to have 60 years of expertise in this field. "Life is about balance," she says. One day she asked if I had any recipes with gin, so I served her this cocktail. As she lifted the glass to her lips, a gentle smile washed over her face as she inhaled. She sipped and said, "Lovely." If you're not a gin lover maybe it's time to give it another try. Gin, made with juniper berries and other botanicals, such as flowers, roots, fruits, and seeds, is the perfect spirit to infuse into tiki drinks like Rosemary Lemonade. The gin's smooth, cheerful crispness balances out the sweetness of the lemonade and syrup while complimenting the subtle flavors of the rosemary.

2½ ounces Bombay Sapphire® or other dry gin

2 ounces Lynn's Lemonade (page 33)

1 ounce Rosemary Lemon Syrup (page 24)

1 sprig rosemary for garnish

1 lemon wheel (page 15) for garnish

Combine the gin, lemonade, and syrup in a cocktail shaker with ice. Shake for 10 seconds, and then strain into a rocks glass filled with ice. Garnish with the rosemary sprig and lemon wheel or twist, as shown on the table of contents page.

note: For a different and equally refreshing take on this cocktail, try making it with Hendrick's gin, which features soft botanical notes of cooling cucumbers and soothing rose petals.

Santorini Spritzer

This cocktail, made with ouzo, a Greek aperitif flavored with anise and other herbs, is dedicated to Uncle Michael Alexandrou, an international businessman and world traveler, and the Dapontes family, a lovely and wild Greek family I grew up with. They hail from the island of Kythera, said to be the birthplace of Aphrodite, goddess of love. The island served as a crossroads for sailors and merchants, creating a melting pot of cultures influenced by the Ottoman and Venetian empires, clearly evident in the island's architecture. Lemons, oranges, and fennel all grow here, where the shimmering Aegean Sea caresses beautiful beaches dotted with thatched tiki bars. Polynesian culture has made its way even to the Greek islands! Enjoy this refreshing cocktail as Apollo's chariot sinks into the sea.

1 ounce ouzo

1 ounce limoncello

2 ounces Fennel Orange Puree (page 27)

tonic water, chilled

1 Mandarin orange wedge with peel (page 15) for garnish

Fill a Collins glass with ice. Add the ouzo, limoncello, and puree. Top with tonic water. Stir, and then garnish with the orange wedge.

Seascape Almond Slush

The Seascape, a 14-room boutique motel on Singer Island, Florida, is owned by two remarkable hosts who inspired the Almond Slush. Thanks for the hospitality, Alicia and Hagan. This one's for you!

¾ ounce light rum

¾ ounce spiced rum

½ ounce amaretto

⅛ ounce Cointreau

1½ ounces mango nectar

1½ ounces pineapple juice

1½ dashes Stirrings® or other blood orange bitters

½ Mandarin orange, peeled and segmented

1 edible orchid (page 17) for garnish

1 mango spear (page 18) for garnish

In a blender, combine the light rum, spiced rum, amaretto, Cointreau, mango nectar, pineapple juice, bitters, Mandarin orange, and 1 cup of ice. Blend on high until smooth. Pour into a chilled highball glass and garnish with the orchid and mango spear.

note: You can also serve this drink on the rocks, as shown here, instead of blending it.

Tahiti 5-Oh!

You can't mention tiki without mentioning Hawaii. For 12 seasons, from 1968 to 1980, the popular *Hawaii Five-O* TV show was shot on location in the Aloha State, proving that a police procedural set in a tropical paradise can survive just like good tiki drinks, which were enormously popular during the show's run. Perhaps not coincidentally, the tiki craze has reemerged right along with the reboot of the series. A perfect blend of five ingredients makes this tropical delight that playfully refers to the TV show a great refreshing summer cocktail. Just don't get into trouble after you have one. Otherwise, "Book 'em, Danno!"

2½ ounces Pineapple Vanilla Vodka (page 34)

2½ ounces coconut rum

½ ounce blue curaçao

3 ounces Coco López or other cream of coconut

6 ounces pineapple juice

2 Drunken Pineapple Wedges (page 21) for garnish

In a blender, combine the vodka, rum, curaçao, cream of coconut, pineapple juice, and 2 cups of ice. Blend on high until smooth. Divide between two Collins glasses. Garnish with the pineapple wedges and serve with paper umbrellas and straws.

Serves 2 because it's always better to have a partner in crime.

Tutu's Slush & Flush

Tutu is an endearing Hawaiian term for grandmother, but it can refer to both genders. Dried plums are an excellent natural source of vitamins and fiber, and are great for skin and bone health, but most people think of their grandparents when they hear the word *prune*. Years ago, while spending the winter months in South Florida, I met many wonderful grandparents from all over the world. Since they and my Grandmother Fiorita served as the inspiration for this cocktail, I asked them to taste test it. No one guessed that prune juice is one of the ingredients. They absolutely loved it, so this cocktail is dedicated respectfully to all of the wise ones who lovingly paved the way for us.

2½ ounces Tito's vodka

3½ ounces prune juice

½ ounce agave nectar

juice of half a lemon

1 lemon wheel (page 15) for garnish

In a cocktail shaker, combine the vodka, juice, and nectar. Add some ice and shake for about 10 seconds. Strain and pour into a martini glass half filled with crushed ice. Garnish with the lemon wheel and serve immediately.

Very Berry Brazil

First distilled by the Portuguese in the 1500s, cachaça is a spirit distilled from sugar cane and aged in wood barrels for up to 12 months. It's also the most widely consumed liquor in Brazil. When paired with fresh blueberries from a farmers market and mint plucked right from the garden, the result is a perfectly balanced summer cocktail.

3 fresh mint leaves

8–10 large blueberries

½ ounce agave nectar

¼ ounce lime juice

2½ ounces cachaça

1 sprig mint for garnish

Place the mint leaves, blueberries, nectar, and juice in a rocks glass. Muddle to release the flavor from the mint and the juice of the berries. Fill the glass with crushed ice and add the cachaça. Tumble into a cocktail shaker and shake for about 5 seconds. Return the mixture to the glass and garnish with a fresh mint sprig and an optional lime twist.

TIKITINIS

TIKI-INSPIRED MARTINIS ARE FUN, SEXY, AND SOPHISTICATED WHETHER served straight up in a martini glass or on the rocks. Tikitinis make a statement and set the mood for a memorable evening. When hosting an event or gathering, prepare a batch in advance, and store them in sealed glass containers in the refrigerator. Then set the scene before your guests arrive. Lay banana leaves diagonally along your bar top as a tropical mat or instead of a cocktail tray. Cut your fruit and garnishes ahead of time, and arrange them in coconut cups placed on the banana leaves. Put bamboo skewers, drink parasols, and straws in colorful tiki mugs. Edible tropical orchids are also a great touch. Wicker or thatched baskets can disguise an old ice bucket. Set up your chilled martini glasses on the banana leaves just before your guests arrive. Finally, you'll want to play some tunes—like Israel Kamakawiwoʻole's "Over the Rainbow" or Gabby Pahinui's "Hiʻilawe"—while you sip your tropical drinks and enjoy!

Chocolate Divatini

This is the dessert version of the Raspberry Jalapeño Tikitini (page 101). The simple addition of dark chocolate liqueur transforms this cocktail into a decadent dessert martini. It sounds like a chick drink, but a few boat captains who shall remain nameless love it. (They asked me not to reveal their identities. You know how men can be.)

⅛ cup fresh raspberries, plus extra for garnish

¼ ounce Chambord™ or other raspberry liqueur

2 ounces Pineapple Jalapeño Vodka (page 34)

1 ounce Godiva® or other dark chocolate liqueur

splash of pineapple juice

Rinse the raspberries and place in a cocktail shaker. Add the raspberry liqueur and muddle the berries to release the juice. Add the vodka, chocolate liqueur, pineapple juice, and some ice. Cover and shake for about 15 seconds. Strain and pour into a chilled martini glass. Garnish with one or two raspberries for an added pop of freshness. For a little extra kick, add an optional jalapeño slice to the garnish.

Hot Cucumber Tikitini

Recent studies are declaring the cucumber one of the world's healthiest foods. Cucumbers are said to help prevent cancer and to reduce the incidence of cardiovascular disease. Fresh cucumber extracts offer antioxidant and anti-inflammatory benefits along with an abundance of vitamin K, which is essential to building strong bones and helping prevent heart disease. This tikitini is a bit spicy, but the cucumber helps tame this delicious cocktail, which aids digestion and is tastefully smooth. Try it just before dinner.

1 ounce lemon juice

4 cucumber slices, about ⅛ inch thick

¾ ounce agave nectar

2 ounces Cucumber Chile Pepper Vodka (page 32)

Place the lemon juice, three of the cucumber slices, and the nectar into a cocktail shaker. Muddle well. Add some ice and the vodka, and shake for about 10 seconds. Strain and pour into a chilled martini glass. Float a cucumber slice and an optional lemon wheel on top, and enjoy.

Lavender Lemon Tikitini

Eve wanted to get married in Brittany in an old stone church surrounded by a field of lavender. James wanted the wedding to take place in Moorea in French Polynesia. James and Eve had a prewedding cocktail party at the Hula Hut one warm spring afternoon, and of course Eve got her way. This cocktail pays homage to Eve's inevitable victory. May she and James drink happily ever after!

1 tablespoon sugar
for rimming

5 ounces Tito's vodka

2 ounces Lavender Lemon
Syrup (page 23)

1 ounce lemon juice

2 sprigs fresh culinary
lavender for garnish

Rim two chilled martini glasses with sugar and set aside.

Fill a cocktail shaker with ice. Add the vodka, syrup, and lemon juice. Shake for about 10 seconds, then strain and divide into the chilled martini glasses. Float a sprig of fresh lavender in each glass for a beautiful finish.

Serves 2 in honor of James and Eve.

note: Lavender belongs to the mint family. Although you can use most varieties of lavender in cocktails, culinary lavenders, such English lavender, offer a sweeter fragrance, which increases the flavor profile of the drink. Using the fragrant leaves and stems works, but the purple flowers will give your cocktails a subtle citrus flavor. Lavender grows well in dry, sunny climes, so place a pot on your windowsill or plant some in a sunny spot in your garden.

Raspberry Jalapeño Tikitini

Raspberries are loaded with vitamin C, manganese, and fiber. They also contain a compound that may help manage obesity and type 2 diabetes. There are more than 200 species of raspberries, but I stick to the mature red varieties like the European Red. Many years ago a dear friend gave me a jar of homemade raspberry jalapeño jam. That amazing combination of hot and sweet inspired this cocktail. The vodka infusion used in this cocktail is wonderful with the addition of sweet ripe pineapple. Get creative and add dark chocolate to create the perfect dessert martini in the Chocolate Divatini (page 97).

⅛ cup fresh raspberries, plus extra for garnish

½ ounce Chambord or other raspberry liqueur

2 ounces Pineapple Jalapeño Vodka (page 34)

1½ ounces pineapple juice

Rinse the raspberries and place them in a cocktail shaker. Add the raspberry liqueur and muddle the berries to release their juice. Add the vodka, pineapple juice, and some ice. Shake for about 15 seconds. Strain into a chilled martini glass and garnish with a couple of raspberries for an added pop of freshness.

The Speedy Rodriguez

Many years ago while spending a winter in Playa del Carmen, Mexico, I frequented a small café where a small Mayan man carefully stacked a pyramid of espresso cups to symbolize the Mayan pyramids of Tulum. He climbed on a stool and slowly poured a bottle of something extremely potent, like Mexican moonshine, over the coffee cups, beginning at the top and working his way down to fill every cup. Then he ignited the pyramid, and the crowd went mad! We nicknamed him Speedy Rodriguez. He did several shows a night and inspired me to create this cocktail. You can also enjoy this cocktail after dinner in place of an espresso.

3 ounces espresso

2 ounces Coco Loco Infusion (page 31)

1 lemon twist (page 15) for garnish

Prepare the espresso in advance using an espresso maker. Set it aside and let it cool to room temperature. (You can also use espresso made with instant espresso powder if you don't have access to an espresso maker).

Add 1 cup of ice to a cocktail shaker. Pour in the espresso and the Coco Loco Infusion. Shake vigorously for about 10 seconds, then strain into a chilled martini glass. Garnish with a lemon twist.

note: *For more of a dessert-style presentation, rim the glass with brown sugar.*

Tahitian Lemon Drop

As the sun settles into the horizon, casting its golden amber glow, the essence of orange, pineapple, and vanilla of this sultry cocktail makes the perfect end to a perfect day.

1 large lemon

½ tablespoon brown sugar for rimming

1½ ounces Pineapple Vanilla Vodka (page 34)

1½ ounces Tuaca®

⅜ ounce triple sec

Slice the lemon into halves. Press and strain the juice from one of the halves into a large cocktail shaker and set aside. Slice a thin wheel from the remaining half and set aside for garnish.

Rub the squeezed lemon half around the edge of a chilled martini glass, then rim with brown sugar and set aside.

Add the vodka, Tuaca, triple sec, and some ice to the shaker, and shake for 10 to 12 seconds. Strain and pour into the martini glass, and float a lemon wheel atop the cocktail.

note: Tuaca is an Italian citrus liqueur flavored with vanilla.

TAHITI

French Polynesia consists of 118 islands and atolls spread over five archipelagos. In 1767, Samuel Wallis was the first European to visit Tahiti. The next year famed explorer Captain Cook arrived, followed later by whalers, missionaries, and the French, who ultimately took ownership of the islands. Notable French painter Paul Gauguin lived here, and today you'll find a small museum dedicated to his work. Millions of travelers visit each year and encounter the iconic tiki, a large wood carving representing authentic Polynesian culture. Tikis, in which the drinks originated, often mark boundaries of important and sacred sites. Polynesian clans, who considered themselves descendants of Polynesian gods, dominated the islands. Many tikis today represent these ancient gods.

Tahiti's Mai Tai is the most famous of the island's tropical libations. Less well known but just as delicious are the Pina Lagoon, Banana Coralia, and Maeva. If you're lucky, you may be served a cocktail garnished with a tiare flower. These sweet-scented flowers truly embody the island's spirit. But if you decide to pluck it from your glass and wear it behind your ear, make sure you understand proper placement. Wearing the tiare flower on your left ear means you're married. On your right ear signifies that you're single and searching for a mate.

Tahiti Spice Tikitini

The Tahitian vanilla bean is the queen of vanilla. Every summer, Tahiti celebrates Vanilla Week, a delightful festival that includes trips to vanilla farms so you can learn how the world's best quality vanilla is produced, prepared, and transformed. Tahitian vanilla has unique aromatic qualities, and its limited supply is highly sought worldwide. The Tahitian vanilla bean originated from a hybrid between West Indian and Mexican beans, resulting in a rare bean with deep fruit and floral aromas. This cocktail contains an exotic blend of vanilla, ginger, and cinnamon. When paired with citrus and chilled, it's extremely refreshing on a hot summer day.

2 ounces Tahitian Blend Infusion (page 35)

1 ounce orange juice

1 ounce pomegranate juice

½ ounce lime juice

1 orange twist (page 15) for garnish

In a large cocktail shaker, combine the infusion, orange juice, pomegranate juice, and lime juice. Add ice and shake for 10 to 15 seconds. Strain into a chilled martini glass and garnish with an orange twist, or serve on the rocks in a wine glass with an additional lime wedge and paper parasol.

tiki tip: The best way to use a vanilla bean is to split the delicate pod in half, carefully exposing the seeds, which are what gives a cocktail or dish the vanilla flavor. For tropical infusions, use the entire pod.

CUCKOO FOR

COCONUTS

GROWN IN THE TROPICS AND SUBTROPICS, COCONUTS ARE ONE OF THE MOST versatile fruits on the planet. You can use every part of this amazing fruit, and an immature coconut contains a large amount of water that you can drink. A good coconut should feel heavy for its size. Shake the coconut. You should hear plenty of juice inside. This is the coconut water, and the more the better. Finally, inspect the outer shell of the coconut. The shell should be clean and brown. Discard any nuts that are discolored, cracked, or don't have any water inside. To open the coconut, the best tools to use (avoid using machetes and hatchets; you're just asking for trouble). With the claw part of the hammer, pierce the top of the coconut (the part that looks like a miniature bowling bowl with the three "eyes"). Continue to pierce the nut until the top breaks open. Be careful not to spill the delicious coconut water inside. You'll want to drink this. Remove the water and then use the hammer again to break the shell into pieces, giving you access to the delicious white flesh inside.

Mature coconuts often are harvested and processed for a healthy oil used in cooking and skin care products. The flesh, meanwhile, is delicious raw or toasted. Coconut milk and oil are used in soaps and other beauty products, and the shells can become jewelry and home decor.

In some cultures, the coconut palm is called the tree of life and revered for its healing properties. It's the most consumed natural product for healthy living. Try the recipes in this chapter to capture some of that healing energy. If you believe that less is more and fresh is best, then you definitely will be cuckoo for coconuts after you try these cocktails. Make your guests feel special by serving these drinks in monogrammed coconut cups, which make great mementoes.

Brazilian Breezer

You will absolutely flip over this cocktail. The freshness of the cucumber combined with the tropical taste of coconut will leave you wanting more. This recipe is dedicated to my Brazilian friend Adrian, whom I met years ago while vacationing in Fort Lauderdale, Florida. We met at a tiny tiki bar on a beautiful sandy beach at the Marriott Harbor Beach Resort, where Adrian was working as a bartender. He made me a refreshing concoction of muddled cucumber, rum, pineapple juice, and club soda. It was tasty, but I'm more of a tequila girl, so back in Montauk I started experimenting. With a few cucumbers muddled in my Coco Loco Infusion, the delicious and refreshing Brazilian Breezer was born!

5 cucumber slices, about ⅛-inch thick

2 ounces pineapple juice

2 ounces Coco Loco Infusion (page 31)

In a large rocks glass, place 4 cucumber slices and the pineapple juice. Muddle the cucumber to release its flavor. Fill the glass with crushed ice and add the Coco Loco Infusion. Transfer to a cocktail shaker, shake for about 10 seconds, and return to the glass. Garnish with the remaining cucumber wheel and optional lime and pineapple wedges.

Chile Pepper Coconut Cooler

Chile peppers range from mild to throat scorching. In general, the smaller the pepper, the hotter it is. Be *extremely* careful when handling them, particularly in the kitchen. Use gloves—and *don't* touch your eyes after handling them. All peppers have either sweet or hot flesh. Bells and pimentos are sweet, while chiles are hot. The heat comes from an oily substance called capsaicin, located in yellow sacs on the inside wall of the pepper pod. As long as these sacs aren't broken, a hot pepper will remain mild. But rough handling during harvest or packing, or biting a pepper can increase its hotness. Capsaicin spreads into the pepper's seeds, so remove them to turn down the heat. Always choose chiles that are glossy, firm, and free of soft spots or blemishes. Keep them in sealed plastic bags in the refrigerator for up to 1 week, or freeze them by slitting them open, removing the seeds, and placing them in freezer bags. In this unique cocktail, the cucumber cools the heat of the chile pepper, and the natural sweetness of the coconut water and pineapple juice offer a smooth balance. I serve this cocktail in a coconut shell drinking cup, but you can use a large rocks glass.

2 ounces Cucumber Chile Pepper Vodka (page 32)

3 ounces coconut water

¼ ounce pineapple juice

1 cucumber slice, about ⅛-inch thick, for garnish

Combine the vodka, coconut water, and pineapple juice in a cocktail shaker with ice. Shake for about 5 seconds, then strain into a coconut shell, coconut cup, or large rocks glass filled with crushed ice. Float a cucumber slice on top and serve with a straw.

note: If your palate overheats from a fiery chile pepper, never drink water. The best remedy is to consume dairy products, such as milk, yogurt, sour cream, or ice cream.

Coco Loco Cocktail

One afternoon at the Hula Hut, my friend Dianne asked me to create a cocktail with tequila and coconut, her two favorite ingredients—and mine! A petite and gorgeous *mamacita*, Dianne loves Latin music and a good time. Some of my customers jokingly call me "Dr. Lynn, Medicine Woman" after I've intuitively prescribed a custom cocktail for them. I just have a sense for what people want. After experimenting with several different tropical fruits, I decided to keep it simple. Just a tiny bit of pineapple juice and lime is all it took. Dianne absolutely flipped over this one, and it's now one of the top sellers at the bar. You can often catch Dianne and the gang enjoying several Coco Loco's in our Zen Den. Thanks for your inspiration, chica!

2 ounces Coco Loco Infusion (page 31)

2 ounces pineapple juice

¼ ounce lime juice

1 pineapple wedge (page 20) for garnish

Fill a rocks glass with ice. Add the Coco Loco Infusion, pineapple juice, and lime juice. Stir, then garnish with a pineapple wedge.

Cocomint Cooler

An exotic and stunning locale, Thailand is known for its tropical beaches, ancient ruins, and sacred shrines to the Buddha, who graces my Hula Hut as well. Thai cuisine, one of the most popular in the world, relies on fresh, local ingredients like delicious coconuts and fragrant mint, both featured in this cocktail. If you're ever in Thailand, take the time to visit the many food courts, markets, and award-winning restaurants. You can even take various culinary tours and cooking classes . . . while sipping on Thai-crafted tropical cocktails like this one. The combination of coconut and mint makes it extremely refreshing.

4 mint leaves

1 lime wedge (page 15)

¾ ounce agave nectar

1½ ounces premium light rum

½ ounce coconut rum

3 ounces coconut water

1 sprig mint for garnish

Place the mint leaves, lime wedge, and agave nectar in a cocktail shaker. Muddle to release the flavors from the leaves and the juice from the lime. Add the light rum, coconut rum, coconut water, and some ice. Shake for about 10 seconds. Strain into a Collins glass filled with ice. Garnish with the mint sprig and serve with a straw. Alternately you can serve this drink in a coconut shell garnished with a lime wheel and paper parasol for an even more tropical feel.

COCONUT WATER

Coconut water has exploded in popularity, but it's been around forever. Because it's low in calories and has no cholesterol, and one serving has more potassium than four bananas, this naturally refreshing drink adds the perfect touch to coconut cocktails. Just don't drink too much of it. Remember the movie *Castaway*? Chuck Noland—the Tom Hanks character stranded on a remote island littered with coconuts—reminds us that coconut water is a natural laxative. Coconut water also aids in weight loss because the water's naturally rich properties help suppress the appetite. Of course, we can't talk about coconut water in a cocktail book without mentioning its use as a hangover cure. Drinking coconut water after you've had one too many will settle your stomach while replacing essential electrolytes that you may have lost from dehydration (or after paying homage to the porcelain god). More importantly, coconut water will replace those lost minerals and vital nutrients much better than sports drinks can. If that isn't enough to convince you to drink coconut water, this natural liquid is also said to reduce blood pressure.

Coconut Cooler

For those dog days of summer, this cocktail is extremely refreshing. The gin helps cut the natural sweetness of the coconut by adding some herbal sharpness to the mixture. You'll love it.

2 ounces premium dry gin

3 ounces coconut water

1 ounce coconut milk

¼ ounce agave nectar

1 lime wheel (page 15) for garnish

In a cocktail shaker combine the gin, coconut water, coconut milk, and agave nectar. Add some ice and shake for about 10 seconds. Strain into a coconut shell drinking cup or large rocks glass filled with crushed ice. Garnish with a lime wheel.

tiki tip: Serving cocktails in natural coconut shell drinking cups adds an authentic tropical touch to any tiki gathering. They're inexpensive, and you easily can find them online. For an intimate cocktail party or special event, order monogrammed coconut cups for your guests to take home with them. It's a nice personal touch. You can buy them from CoconutKing.com or other online retailers.

Lavender Coconut Cocktail

French Polynesia has more than 50 airports, so getting there is relatively easy. You can practically land on the island of your choice. No wonder almost 200,000 visitors arrive every year to frolic under the sun. Bring your sunscreen and a big appetite because the food in French Polynesia is delicious and often prepared using local produce such as coconuts and other fresh fruits and vegetables. The islands don't have any poisonous snakes or insects, although the mosquitos bite, as might the occasional sea turtle or shark. Best to belly up to the bar and enjoy the shimmering sea from a distance with this cocktail in your hand. The flavors of lavender and coconut water perfectly balance to result in an aromatic, soothing, and hydrating cocktail. Lie back and savor this one.

2 ounces Tito's vodka

4 ounces coconut water

1 ounce Lavender Lemon Syrup (page 23)

1 sprig fresh lavender for garnish

In a cocktail shaker, combine the vodka, coconut water, syrup, and some ice. Shake for about 10 seconds, then strain into a coupe filled with crushed ice. Garnish with the sprig of fresh lavender and enjoy.

FROZEN

DELIGHTS

RUM AND PINEAPPLE JUICE FREQUENTLY WERE SERVED TOGETHER IN TROPICAL climes where sugar cane and pineapples grew, but commercially viable ice didn't become available in the Caribbean until 1807. Most classic tiki cocktails are muddled and stirred or shaken—which isn't surprising because many of them originated before the blender became a common household item. Stephen Poplawski patented the first blender in 1922, the same year as the first written reference appears for that most iconic tiki drink, the Piña Colada. Cream of coconut didn't hit the market for several more decades, though. Ramón López Irizarry, a professor of agriculture at the University of Puerto Rico, discovered how to produce it commercially in 1954, paving the way for the Piña Colada recipe that everyone knows and loves today. The concoction contains light aged rum, coconut milk, and fresh pineapple juice. Tiki versions of other classic frozen drinks, such as the daiquiri and margarita, make use of blended fruit. Fresh fruit is always better than sugary store-bought purees or mixers, but a little bit of Coco López goes a long way. If fresh fruits aren't in season, then use unsweetened frozen fruits as an alternative. It's also better to add the ice after the measured ingredients to keep the ice from melting too quickly. Always secure the lid on the blender before you begin pulsing, and never remove it while it's running. Always start your blender on a medium speed for a few seconds before increasing to higher speeds to achieve the desired consistency. Choose fun and unique glassware, and don't forget the tiki couture tips (page 13), including colorful fruits and garnishes, tropical drink parasols, and even sparklers for that celebratory cocktail.

Banana Hammock

The popular and iconic 1980s television series *Miami Vice* inspired this cocktail. The drink is sexy and sophisticated and takes after the Miami Vice Cocktail—itself a combination of a Rum Runner and the Piña Colada—which popped up in tiki bars all over South Florida during the show's heyday. This is my twist on that retro classic.

1 ripe banana

1½ ounces light rum

1 ounce coconut rum

½ ounce dark rum

1 ounce Coco López or other cream of coconut

2 ounces pineapple juice

½ ounce lime juice

⅛ ounce grenadine

¼ cup blackberries

¼ cup vanilla ice cream

Peel half of the banana, cut the half in half, spear the quarter with a 4-inch bamboo skewer, and set aside for garnish.

In a blender, combine the the remaining ingredients and the rest of the banana with 1¼ cups of ice. Blend until smooth, then pour into a hurricane glass. Lay the speared banana garnish atop the cocktail and serve with a straw.

note: For a nice layered effect, float a little extra dark rum atop the drink before you serve it.

Caribbean Comfort Cocktail

This drink is off-the-charts delicious.

1 ripe banana

2 ounces Caribbean
Comfort Infusion (page 31)

½ ounce coconut rum

1½ ounces pineapple juice

½ cup vanilla ice cream

½ ounce dark rum

whipped cream

¼ teaspoon
ground cinnamon

1 Drunken Pineapple
Wedge (page 21)
for garnish

Peel the banana, cut it in half, and place one half in a blender. Add the Caribbean Comfort Infusion, coconut rum, pineapple juice, ice cream, and 1½ cups of ice. Blend on high until smooth, then pour into a Collins glass. Float the dark rum on top of the cocktail, and top with whipped cream and a sprinkle of cinnamon. Garnish with a Drunken Pineapple Wedge and the other banana half, and serve with a straw.

note: *You can use fat-free frozen yogurt instead of ice cream for a lighter version of the cocktail.*

Caribbean Dreamsicle

Don't be fooled by this surprisingly smooth and sweet treat, which I, not the ice cream man, am bringing to you.

1½ ounces Pineapple
Vanilla Vodka (page 34)

¾ ounce Tuaca

½ ounce Cointreau

2 ounces orange juice

1 small scoop of vanilla ice
cream, approximately ½ cup

whipped cream

1 orange wedge (page 15)
for garnish

In a blender, combine the vodka, Tuaca, Cointreau, orange juice, ice cream, and 1¼ cups of ice. Blend on high until smooth, then pour into a Collins glass. Top with whipped cream, garnish with an orange wedge, and serve with a straw.

tiki tip: For that extra presentation sparkle, put a sparkler in the drink, and light it before serving. Just make sure to set it on an angle so that you don't wind up with ashes in your cocktail.

Honeydew Daiquiri

Every woman should have a "honey do" list, and this cocktail should top it. You come home from a hard day of work, and your tall, dark, chiseled man is wearing nothing but a sarong and a smile and lovingly hands you a Honeydew Daiquiri made from scratch. A girl can dream, can't she? But seriously, nothing screams summertime like the aroma of sweet, ripe melon. You're going to love this one.

½ cup fresh honeydew melon chunks, plus 1 extra for garnish

2 ounces Pineapple Vanilla Vodka (page 34)

½ ounce melon liqueur

3 ounces pineapple juice

½ ounce lime juice

½ cup vanilla ice cream

If you use a fresh honeydew melon, cut it in half, scoop out the seeds, and discard them. Use a melon baller or spoon to remove the flesh from the melon. See page 19 for more on melon preparation. You also can use fresh honeydew melon chunks available at most grocery stores.

In a blender, add the melon chunks, vodka, melon liqueur, pineapple juice, lime juice, ice cream, and 1 ½ cups of ice. Blend until smooth, then pour into a footed pilsner or hurricane glass. Stab the remaining melon chunk with a drink umbrella, place across the top of the glass, and serve with a straw, or lay the chunk across the glass and add an edible orchid next to it. .

note: You can use fat-free frozen yogurt instead of ice cream for a lighter version of the cocktail.

Lono

In traditional Hawaiian culture, Lono is the god of fertility and peace. This cocktail earned its name after not one but two couples told me that they conceived their first child after downing a few of these potent concoctions.

1½ ounces coconut rum

1½ ounces light rum

½ ounce Frangelico or other hazelnut liqueur

3 ounces mango nectar

2 ounces Coco López or other cream of coconut

¼ fresh banana

¼ ounce dark rum

whipped cream

1 ounce shredded coconut

In a blender, combine the coconut and light rums, hazelnut liqueur, mango nectar, cream of coconut, banana, and 1½ cups of ice. Blend on high until smooth. Fill a footed pilsner or hurricane glass with crushed ice, then pour in the cocktail. Float the dark rum on top. Top with whipped cream and a sprinkle of shredded coconut.

PLEASE DON'T TAKE THE TIKI MUGS

According to many reports, tiki mugs are the second most stolen novelty item in bars, right behind by the shiny copper mugs used for Moscow Mules. The Hula Hut doesn't serve drinks in tiki mugs, but bartenders around the globe should keep their eyes on their decorative mugs and even tiki bowls after serving them to patrons, who may want more than just a dazzling, delicious drink. These iconic glazed ceramic vessels with evil or funny faces make for great collectible souvenirs in the home bar, especially if they're vintage tiki mugs from historic Hawaiian and Polynesian restaurants and bars. At the height of the tiki craze, the two leading manufacturers of treasured tiki mugs and bowls were Orchids of Hawaii and Otagiri Mercantile Company. Other rare vessels that command high prices today include tiki mugs that resemble Easter Island moai or Fu Manchu, and Trader Vic's Mai Tai Joe mug, commonly known as the Suffering Bastard, named after a cocktail of the same name. Most tiki-themed restaurants and bars today serve tropical libations from replica tiki mugs and bowls. Nevertheless, keep an eye out!

Toasted Coconut

Hold on to your coconuts, this cocktail is a knockout! The scent of cinnamon adds a feeling of calm, but don't let your guard down: the 151 rum packs some serious punch!

3 ounces Caribbean
Comfort Infusion
(page 31)

1½ ounces amaretto

1 ounce 151 rum

3 ounces Coco López or
other cream of coconut

4 ounces orange juice

2 ounces pineapple juice

whipped cream

2 tablespoons toasted
coconut flakes

2 orange wheels
(page 15) for garnish

In a blender, combine the Caribbean Comfort Infusion, amaretto, rum, cream of coconut, orange juice, pineapple juice, and 3 cups of ice. Blend on high until smooth, then divide between two small hurricane glasses. Top with whipped cream and a sprinkle of coconut flakes. Garnish each glass with an orange wheel, and serve with a straw.

note: Most grocery stores carry toasted coconut flakes. If you can't find them, here's how to make your own: Preheat the oven to 400°F. Sprinkle a thin layer of shredded coconut—found in the baking section of most grocery stores—evenly on a large cookie sheet. Place the sheet on the top rack in the oven for 8 to 12 minutes or until the coconut turns golden brown. Be sure to keep an eye on it while it's baking so it doesn't burn. Let cool to room temperature, transfer to a sealed container, and store in a cool, dry place for up to a week.

BLOODY

PARADISE

EVERY SATURDAY AND SUNDAY AT NOON, THE HULA HUT PRESENTS A spectacular Bloody Mary bar. It offers a delicious opportunity for guests to get creative while enjoying a delicious cocktail. We stage a variety of tomato juices and blends, including heirloom tomato, Clamato®, V8®, and Zing Zang® (a New Orleans favorite). We also feature more than 20 different hot sauces and spices, like Slap Ya Mama®, Bubba's Butt Blaster, Old Bay®, and a collection of curries. Mason jars contain an array of condiments from horseradish pickles and stuffed olives to okra and pickled garlic scapes (the curly flower stalks of garlic plants)—all from the Montauk Farmers Market. You can also have your drink and eat it too by adding fresh jumbo shrimp, crispy bacon, chilled crab claws, or vibrant caprese skewers. The sky's the limit when it comes to Bloody Marys, so have fun setting up your own Bloody Mary bar for your guests. It gives them a great chance to interact, and they'll love it. When you think tiki, you probably don't think Bloody Marys, but the recipes in this chapter all have a delicious tropical twist. After all, who doesn't love paradise?

Bloody Mango

Did you know that the mango is the most popular fruit in the world? This tropical symbol of love is available year round. According to the National Mango Board, the majority of mangos sold in America come from Mexico, Peru, Ecuador, Brazil, Guatemala, and Haiti. Varieties of the fruit include the Ataulfo, Francis, Haden, Keitt, Kent, and Tommy Atkins—so there's a version for everyone.

2 ounces Tito's vodka

4 ounces tomato juice

3 ounces mango nectar

⅛ teaspoon lemon juice

⅛ teaspoon Sriracha

1 mango spear (page 18) for garnish

Fill a Collins glass with ice. Add the vodka, tomato juice, mango nectar, lemon juice, and Sriracha. Tumble into a shaker, then return the mixture to the glass. Repeat. Garnish with a fresh mango spear for a pop of color and a healthy snack while you sip your drink.

Bloody Pineapple

This one is definitely unique—it's not even close to what you'd expect in a Bloody Mary. The scent of curry will hit you before the first sip, then the sweet sensation of pineapple and the cool lime create an interesting tropical combination and cocktail that's easy to enjoy.

2 ounces premium silver rum

4 ounces V8 juice

2 ounces pineapple juice

¼ ounce lime juice

⅛ teaspoon curry powder

3 or 4 dashes hot sauce

1 fresh pineapple wedge (page 20) for garnish

Fill a Collins glass with ice. Add the rum, V8 juice, pineapple juice, lime juice, curry powder, and hot sauce. Tumble into a shaker, then return the mixture to the glass. Garnish with the pineapple wedge.

note: *Every hot sauce is different. For this recipe I prefer Texas Pete. It's fine to use another brand, but I prefer a forward pepper and cayenne flavor.*

Bloody Thailand

The surprising flavor of peanuts in this Bloody Mary offers an unexpected yet interestingly pleasant twist that will leave your guests wanting more.

2 ounces Cucumber Vodka (page 32)

4 ounces tomato juice

1 ounce Bangkok Padang™ Peanut Sauce

¾ ounce Cucumber, Cilantro & Jalapeño Puree (page 25)

¼ ounce lime juice

¼ teaspoon Sriracha

1 cucumber wheel (page 15) for garnish

Fill a Collins glass with ice, then add the vodka, tomato juice, peanut sauce, puree, lime juice, and Sriracha. Tumble into a shaker, then return the mixture to the glass. Repeat, then garnish with a cucumber wheel.

note: Peanut sauce is available in the international foods aisle at most grocery stores. Also, if you have a peanut allergy, obviously you should avoid this cocktail. If not, you should enjoy it as often as you like!

Ginger Island Bloody

The lemongrass and ginger in this delightful cocktail will make you think of Thailand as well, but in a deliciously different way. The combination of sweetness and spice with just a hint of earthy, tangy soy flavor gives this bloody what I like to call a Pacific Rim twist.

2 ounces Ginger Lemongrass Vodka (page 32)

3 ounces tomato juice

2 ounces Lynn's Lemonade (page 33)

1 dash soy sauce

⅛ teaspoon ground black pepper

1 dill sprig for garnish

1 lemon wheel (page 15) for garnish

Fill a Collins glass with ice, then add the vodka, tomato juice, lemonade, soy sauce, and black pepper. Tumble into a shaker, then return the mixture to the glass. Repeat. Garnish with the dill sprig and lemon wheel.

Mama Fiorita's Bloody Caprese

My beautiful and loving Grandma Fiorita taught me the art of combining flavors and the importance of putting passion into everything I do. When I asked her for certain recipes, she often said, "I don't know, you have to watch me." In true Italian form, she used a pinch of this and a dash of that. A Sunday afternoon favorite featured fresh tomato, mozzarella, and basil drizzled with aged balsamic vinegar as an appetizer before the 10 courses that followed. Fresh and delicious, this drink is a cocktail and appetizer in one and pays tribute to my dear grandmother.

1 lemon

2½ ounces Cucumber Chile Pepper Vodka (page 32)

4 ounces tomato juice

½ teaspoon Old Bayseasoning

¼ teaspoon celery salt

¼ teaspoon fresh ground black pepper

1 Sun Gold cherry tomato for garnish

1 fresh basil leaf for garnish

1 inch mozzarella ball or cube for garnish

½ teaspoon aged balsamic vinegar

Roll the lemon on a hard surface to release the juice from the fruit pulp. Slice it in half, then squeeze or press the juice from one of the halves through a strainer into a Collins glass filled with ice. Add the vodka, tomato juice, Old Bay Seasoning, celery salt, and fresh ground black pepper. Tumble into a shaker, then return the mixture to the glass. Stab a cherry tomato, fresh basil leaf, and a mozzarella ball with a bamboo skewer, and drizzle the balsamic vinegar on the mozzarella. Lay the garnish across the top of the glass.

note: Try fig-infused balsamic vinegar for a sweet and savory flavor profile. For an even stronger flavor punch, use balsamic glaze instead of vinegar.

Pineapple Sage Bloody

The addition of ground sage beautifully balances this cocktail, mellowing and blending the pepper and creating an extremely smooth flavor.

2 ounces Pineapple Jalapeño Vodka (page 34)

3 ounces V8 juice

2 ounces pineapple juice

¼ ounce lemon juice

¼ teaspoon ground sage

2 or 3 dashes hot sauce

1 pineapple wedge (page 20) for garnish

1 sprig sage for garnish

Fill a Collins glass with ice, and then add the vodka, V8 juice, pineapple juice, lemon juice, sage, and hot sauce. Tumble into a shaker, then return the mixture to the glass. Repeat. Garnish with a pineapple wedge and sprig of sage.

note: Every hot sauce is different. For this recipe I prefer Texas Pete. It's fine to use another brand, but ideally you want one with a flavor profile that tastes bold, peppery, and warm.

Sea Candy Bloody

This cocktail can be labor intensive, but it's definitely worth the time and effort. One sip, and you'll taste why. Now you can have your drink and eat it, too!

2 ounces Tito's vodka

4 ounces Clamato juice

2 ounces mango nectar

¼ teaspoon lemon juice

¼ teaspoon soy sauce

1 sea candy scallop skewer (on facing page) for garnish

Fill a Collins glass with ice. Add the vodka, Clamato, mango nectar, lemon juice, and soy sauce. Tumble into a shaker, then return to the glass. Repeat. Garnish with a sea candy scallop skewer and dive in!

note: For a simpler version of this cocktail, you can substitute a lemon wedge for the sea candy scallop skewer.

SEA CANDY SCALLOP SKEWER

It's easier to prepare these skewers in batches ahead of time before serving.

1 bamboo skewer

2 large fresh sea scallops

2 tablespoons Clamato juice

2 tablespoons
mango nectar

1½ tablespoons coconut oil

2½ teaspoons soy sauce

1½ teaspoons lemon juice

2 tablespoons brown sugar

1 dash black pepper

Soak the bamboo skewer in water for about 1 hour.

Rinse the scallops under cold running water and thoroughly pat dry. Spear the scallops on the skewer, place them in a shallow 9 × 9-inch baking pan, and set aside.

In a blender combine the remaining ingredients. Blend on high until the ingredients are mixed thoroughly. Pour the mixture over the scallop skewer, and refrigerate for 3 to 4 hours, flipping the skewer over about once every hour to marinate the scallops evenly. Remove from the refrigerator and set aside.

Heat a well-seasoned iron skillet over medium-high heat. Wipe the pan lightly with coconut oil if necessary to prevent the scallops from sticking. If you're preparing multiple skewers, place the scallops in a single layer, and don't crowd the pan. Let the scallops sear until one side is golden brown and crisp—about 1½ to 2 minutes for an average sea scallop and 2 to 3 minutes for jumbo. Lightly brush the tops of the scallops with some of the marinade as the bottom sears. Using a pair of tongs, carefully turn the skewers to sear the other side. The scallops should be golden-brown and crisp on each side and slightly translucent in the center when fully cooked.

Remove the scallops from the pan and serve as a garnish in the Sea Candy Bloody or as a delicious appetizer. When using them as a cocktail garnish, you may prefer to serve the skewers at room temperature.

CLASSICS

& TWISTS

MY FATHER'S PHILOSOPHY IS "IF IT'S NOT BROKE, DON'T FIX IT." SORRY, DAD, but inspiration lies everywhere. These classic recipes are amazing, but nothing beats some good old-fashioned experimentation to update the classics. In this next chapter, you'll find recipes for some of history's most iconic tiki cocktails along with my interpretations of them that have what I like to call a Pacific Rim twist. Never be afraid to experiment with different flavors to create your own signature cocktails.

Mai Tai

Prohibition pushed American cocktail culture east to Europe and also south into the Caribbean. Ernest Gantt spent time with his rum-running grandfather in Haiti and Cuba and then helped launch what became full-blown tiki culture by opening Don the Beachcomber Cafe in Hollywood, California. (He later changed his name to Donn Beachcomber and then Donn Beach.) Several years before World War II began, Victor Bergeron came across the Don the Beachcomber bar and realized that the idea had legs. Bergeron—later known as Trader Vic—helped spread tiki culture further by founding the famous chain of Trader Vic's restaurant and lounges. Both men claimed credit for inventing this classic cocktail, and they fought over it for years. In the Tahitian language, *maitai* means good, so next time you want a good drink, order a Mai Tai and raise your glass to both Gantt and Bergeron.

1 ounce light rum

½ ounce curaçao

½ ounce orgeat

½ ounce lime juice

1 ounce dark rum

1 maraschino cherry for garnish

Fill a cocktail shaker with ice. Add the light rum, curaçao, orgeat, and lime juice. Shake for about 10 seconds, then strain into a large rocks glass filled with crushed ice. Float the dark rum on top and garnish with a maraschino cherry and optional orange slice.

note: Orgeat syrup is a sweet almond syrup with hints of orange flower water. Proper maraschino cherries are normal cherries infused with maraschino—a liqueur made from cherries—not those neon red monsters that you find in fruit cocktail. You want the ones labeled cocktail cherries.

THE FAMOUS MAI TAI

Everyone has heard of the Mai Tai, but did you know this legendary cocktail comes with its fair share of trivia and controversy? For instance, the drink that put tiki on the map isn't the Mai Tai at all but the Zombie. (More about that later.) Not until Hawaii became a state and the Boeing 747 went into service in 1959 did the Mai Tai begin to take off; it was first attested as an English word for the drink a couple of years later. But did Ernest Gantt or Vic Bergeron introduce it? Today hundreds of variant recipes exist for the Mai Tai because back in the day the original was so top secret that everyone decided to invent his or her own version of it. Regardless of who claims ownership, one thing's for certain: the Mai Tai is delicious, appreciated, and enjoyed in all its various forms.

Swing Tai

This is my twist on the classic Mai Tai. It might not seem at first that the ingredients create a drastic change in taste from the original, but the amaretto, Cointreau, and mango nectar beautifully balance this drink, creating a delicious contemporary cocktail.

1½ ounces light rum

¼ ounce amaretto

¼ ounce Cointreau

1 ounce mango nectar

2 ounces pineapple juice

½ ounce lime juice

1 dash grenadine

¼ ounce dark rum

1 Drunken Pineapple Wedge (page 21) for garnish

1 Traverse City Cherry Bomb (page 14) for garnish

Fill a cocktail shaker with ice. Add the light rum, amaretto, Cointreau, mango nectar, pineapple juice, lime juice, and grenadine. Shake for about 5 seconds, then strain into a large rocks glass filled with crushed ice. Garnish with the pineapple wedge and cherry.

Old-Fashioned

This legendary cocktail—created in Louisville, Kentucky, according to some—always takes me back to my younger days. My parents hosted cocktail parties in the yard during warm summer nights. Upstairs, my cousins and I, supposedly asleep, could hear the sounds of laughter and music playing all night long. My father, a lobsterman, owned a bar and made my mother her favorite cocktail, the Old-Fashioned. The classic recipe calls for bourbon and isn't strictly a tiki drink, although the prevalence of oranges and cherries in modern versions helps give it a tropical twist. My mother still prefers hers made with Scotch, but you can use rye or any other whiskey you like. It's up to you!

2 teaspoons simple syrup

2 orange wedges (page 15)

2 maraschino cherries

2 dashes bitters

1½ ounces Maker's Mark, Bulleit, or other premium bourbon

Place the simple syrup, 1 orange slice, 1 cherry, and the bitters into a large rocks glass. Muddle the fruit to release the juices and to blend the syrup and bitters. Fill the glass with ice, then add the bourbon. Garnish with the remaining orange slice and maraschino cherry.

Island Fashioned

Every classic needs a Caribbean or Pacific Rim twist. The cinnamon, nutmeg, and mango nectar in this tropical version of the Old Fashioned provide a soothing remedy for a sore throat as well as the perfect sipping cocktail after dinner.

1 Mandarin orange

3 ounces mango nectar

½ ounce Light Simple Syrup (page 24)

⅛ teaspoon nutmeg

⅛ teaspoon Saigon cinnamon

2½ ounces Maker's Mark or Bulleit bourbon

1 Boudreaux's Bourbon Cherry Bomb (page 14) for garnish

Peel the orange and place three sections in a rocks glass. Add the mango nectar, simple syrup, nutmeg, and cinnamon. Muddle to release the juice of the orange and to blend the nectar, syrup, and spices. Fill the glass with ice, add the bourbon, and transfer to a cocktail shaker. Shake for about 5 seconds, then transfer the contents back to the glass.

With the stem of a paper parasol or a rock candy skewer, spear a Mandarin orange section, and place it in the drink. Garnish with an extra Boudreaux's Bourbon Cherry Bomb if you like.

Pisco Sour

In the mid-1600s, King Philip IV of Spain levied taxes on wine production in Peru, so winemakers turned to moonshining by distilling their grapes in large copper vats. The Peruvians named their new creation after the Port of Pisco, where the liquor was exported (quickly!). Today Peruvians refer to Pisco as their native spirit, which is now made in vineyards along the southwestern coast of Peru using different grape varietals. It's also still produced in copper vats and often crafted in small batches.

2 ounces Pisco Portón®

1 ounce simple syrup

1 ounce lime juice

1 ounce egg white

3 dashes Angostura® bitters

Combine the Pisco, simple syrup, lime juice, and egg white in a blender. Blend on high for about 15 seconds. Add about 5 ice cubes, and pulse the blender five times. Strain into a chilled coupe and add the bitters.

Sweet Basil Pisco

At the Hula Hut, we shake all sorts of drinks to aerate the mixture, thus "waking up" the cocktail. For this drink, shake hard and quick. You're not trying to rock your drink to sleep, so shake it with energy! When shaking, remember to aim the top of your shaker away from your guests. That way, if a dreaded mishap occurs, the liquid shoots behind you instead of hosing down the patron in front of you. This deliciously fresh cocktail is amazing on a hot summer day with seafood or salads.

2 ounces Pisco

½ ounce St-Germain or other elderflower liqueur

2 ounces Watermelon & Basil Puree (page 28)

¾ ounce fresh lemon juice

1 watermelon wedge (page 19) for garnish

1 sprig basil for garnish

In a cocktail shaker, combine the Pisco, elderflower liqueur, puree, and lemon juice. Add several ice cubes and shake for about 5 seconds. Pour into a large chilled rocks glass filled halfway with crushed ice. Garnish with a watermelon wedge and float the basil sprig on top.

Saketini

Sake, an alcohol made from rice, is a favorite in Japan. It's often aged for about six months, during which time it undergoes a fermentation process that resembles brewing beer more than making wine. The more polished or clean the rice, the higher the grade of sake. There are many sakes on the market. Some are designed to be consumed chilled and others consumed warm. When in doubt, select a middle-grade sake, especially for this classic cocktail, which was introduced in the 1960s.

2½ ounces gin

1½ teaspoons sake

1 cocktail olive for garnish

Combine the gin and sake in a cocktail shaker with ice. Shake for about 10 seconds, strain into a chilled martini glass, and garnish with a cocktail olive.

Cucumber Sorbet Saketini

You're going to love the fresh ginger, cold lemon sorbet, and fresh cucumber in my Pacific twist on the Matsuda classic. It's so refreshing.

3 cucumber slices, approximately ⅛ inch thick

¼ ounce lemon juice

½ ounce Light Simple Syrup (page 24)

2 ounces Cucumber Vodka (page 32)

½ ounce dry sake

⅛ teaspoon ginger

1 ball of lemon sorbet, about 2 inches across

1 sprig lemon verbena for garnish

In a cocktail shaker, add the cucumber, lemon juice, and syrup. Muddle well. Add the vodka, sake, ginger, and 1 cup of ice. Shake vigorously for about 10 seconds. Scoop the sorbet into a chilled martini glass. Strain the cocktail over the sorbet and garnish with the sprig of lemon verbena.

Scorpion Bowl

Originating in Honolulu in the 1930s, the Scorpion Bowl traditionally is served in a communal volcano bowl, which at its center has a raised cup in which overproof liquor is ignited to simulate an erupting volcano. Some versions of the bowl made specifically for this cocktail feature scorpions on the rim onto which you can affix various garnishes, such as fresh cherries or pineapple wedges. There are many versions of this festive cocktail, so it's hard to say exactly what the original recipe contained—but I can tell you that it's fun to try them all!

2 ounces gin

2 ounces light rum

2 ounces Tito's vodka

2 ounces 151 rum, divided in halves

2 ounces grenadine

12 ounces orange juice

3 ounces lemon juice

4 pineapple chunks

8 maraschino cherries

In a large pitcher, add the gin, light rum, vodka, 1 ounce of the 151 rum, grenadine, orange juice, lemon juice, pineapple chunks, and cherries. Stir well to blend the flavors. Add 3 cups of crushed ice and transfer to a large scorpion or volcano bowl. If using a volcano bowl, add the remaining 151 rum to the volcano crater, and carefully set it alight. If you don't have a scorpion or volcano bowl with a central crater, simply skip this step, and serve with jumbo straws.

SERVES 2 TO 4

Gemini Bowl

Some people who follow astrology say Scorpios have all the fun, but that's just not true. Gemini is the third astrological sign in the zodiac, named for the Gemini constellation, which honors Castor and Pollux from ancient Greek myth. After the mortal Castor died, Pollux, his immortal twin, asked to share a portion of his immortality so they could remain together. In later versions of the myth, they appear to sailors as St. Elmo's fire. In the zodiac, the sun transits this sign between May 21 and June 21. My birthday is in warm-weather mid-June, which makes sense. For the occasion, I like to serve this variation on the classic Scorpion Bowl. It's so festive, delicious . . . and dangerous at the same time. Don't say I didn't warn you.

2 ounces gin

2 ounces coconut rum

2 ounces light rum

2 ounces 151 rum, divided in halves

2 ounces Tito's vodka

2 ounces grenadine

2 ounces mango nectar

2 ounces passion fruit nectar

2 ounces lemon juice

2 ounces orange juice

2 ounces pineapple juice

4 pineapple chunks

4 Traverse City Cherry Bombs (page 14)

In a large pitcher add the gin, coconut rum, light rum, 1 ounce of the 151 rum, vodka, grenadine, mango nectar, passion fruit nectar, lemon juice, orange juice, and pineapple juice. Stir well to blend the flavors. Refrigerate for 2 to 3 hours before serving.

When ready to serve, add 3 cups of crushed ice to a large volcano or scorpion bowl. Pour the contents of the refrigerated pitcher into the bowl, then float the pineapple chunks and cherries in the bowl. If using a volcano bowl, add the additional 151 rum to the volcano cup in the center, and carefully set it alight. If you don't have a scorpion or volcano bowl with a central crater, simply skip this step. Serve with jumbo straws.

SERVES **2** OR MORE

Singapore Sling

Many recipes claim to be the original Singapore Sling. Chinese bartender Ngiam Tong Boon boasted that he invented the iconic libation in 1915 at the Raffles Hotel in Singapore. The first handwritten recipe disappeared many years ago, and many cocktail buffs dispute the original ingredients. But this is the recipe still served at the Raffles Hotel in Singapore.

1 ½ ounces premium gin

1 ounce B&B® (Bénédictine and Brandy)

1 ounce cherry brandy

1 ounce lime juice

club soda, chilled

1 dash Angostura bitters

Fill a cocktail shaker with ice. Add the gin, B&B, cherry brandy, and lime juice. Shake for about 5 seconds. Strain into a Collins glass filled with crushed ice and top with club soda and a dash of bitters.

note: The original recipe didn't include a garnish.

Singapore Swing

I had a bad experience with gin in my early years, as plenty of people have. But after some time, I gave it another shot. (No pun intended.) I started experimenting by adding fresh fruits and syrups to balance the bitterness of gin, and that's how this twist on the Singapore Sling came about.

1½ ounces gin

¼ ounce Chambord or other raspberry liqueur

Lynn's Lemonade (page 33)

cherry soda

1 dash Angostura bitters

3 or 4 fresh raspberries for garnish

1 lemon wheel (page 15) for garnish

Fill a Collins glass with crushed ice. Add the gin and raspberry liqueur and then equal parts of the lemonade and cherry soda to within ½ inch from the top of the glass.

Rinse the raspberries thoroughly, then float them atop the drink. Garnish with a lemon wheel and serve with a straw.

Zombie

Donn Beachcomber concocted the classic Zombie in 1939. Heavily guarded by its creator, the original recipe had a limit of two per customer because it made him or her feel like, well, you know. Many interpretations of this classic cocktail have appeared over the years, but the below is said to be closest to the original.

1½ ounces gold Puerto Rican rum

1½ ounces Jamaican light rum

¼ teaspoon Pernod®

1 teaspoon grenadine

3 ounces fresh grapefruit juice

1 dash Angostura bitters

1 teaspoon sugar

½ teaspoon cinnamon

1 ounce 151 rum

1 cherry for garnish

In a cocktail shaker filled with ice, add the Puerto Rican and Jamaican rums, Pernod, grenadine, grapefruit juice, bitters, sugar, and cinnamon. Shake for 5 to 10 seconds, then strain into a Collins glass filled with ice. Float the 151 rum on top and garnish with a cherry.

Zydeco Zombie

By now you know that there's a warm place in my heart for southern Louisiana and Cajun culture. My version of the iconic Zombie cocktail has a little *lagniappe* (pronounced *LAN-yap*), a Cajun term meaning "a little something extra." Maybe it's the heat from the hot sauce, one of my rum-soaked cherries, or the unique glass that creates a mysterious glow and will remind you of a full moon on the bayou.

1½ ounces spiced rum

1 ounce light rum

½ ounce dark rum

½ ounce apricot brandy

½ ounce cane syrup

3 ounces grapefruit juice

½ ounce lime juice

¼ teaspoon cinnamon

3 dashes Crystal® or other Louisiana hot sauce

1 dash angostura bitters

1 sugar cane stalk, 8 to 10 inches long, for garnish

1 Traverse City Cherry Bomb (page 14) for garnish

1 cinnamon stalk for garnish

1 lime twist (page 15) for garnish

In a cocktail shaker filled with ice, add the spiced rum, light rum, dark rum, apricot brandy, cane syrup, grapefruit juice, lime juice, cinnamon, hot sauce, and bitters. Shake for 5 seconds, then strain into a mason jar filled with ice, leaving 1 inch at the top of the jar. Garnish with a sugar cane stalk, cinnamon stick, Traverse City Cherry Bomb, and a lime twist.

Play some Chubby Carrier and the Bayou Swamp Band, and *laissez les bons temps rouler!*

tiki tip: For that extra presentation effect, serve this drink in a pint glass with green LED lights in the base. You can find them online at CoolGlow.com.

Acknowledgments

Thanks to: my incredibly talented co-author, James O. Fraioli; James Jayo and the professional team at Sterling Publishing; Karen Wise and her beautiful cocktail photography; Chris for his love and invaluable support, thank you for being my rock; many thanks to the very talented John Shea for your enthusiasm and support; Eamonn, George and Patty, and Jack "the Jackal" for your encouragement and support; Kay and my amazing team of Brian, Sam, and Kirsten, who help me keep my piece of paradise running smoothly; the Grimes family of Montauk for the beautiful beach at Lynn's Hula Hut; Kevin from Island Wide Palm Trees for making the Hut so tropical; Zoe and Thomas (Homeport, Montauk) for your beautiful glassware and decor; Swallow East, Montauk, for giving us shelter from the storm during our photo shoot; Christina Kindwall for your help as well; and last but not least my dear friend Carl Darenberg, who is no longer with us. Thank you for believing in me and for encouraging me not to give up.

Photo Credits

Depositphotos: © vladmoses: 125

iStockphotos: © bhofack2: 85, © kcline: 54, ©kol88: 49, © nata_vkusidey: 50, © nikolay100: 164 (flame), © Roberto A Sanchez: 58, © Valentyn Volkov: 169, © YekoPhotoStudio: 163

Shutterstock: © Shebeko: 155

Courtesy of Wikimedia Foundation: Metropolitan Museum of Art: 105

Recipes & Ingredients Index

Note: Page numbers in parentheses indicate uses of recipe in other recipes.

General Index

Pour spouts, 5
Prohibition, push of American
    cocktail culture elsewhere,
    150
Rimming glasses, 37
Rocks glasses, 9

Scorpion bowls, 162, 165
Shakers, 5, 6
Shaking drinks, 37
Singapore, 166

Skewers, 5
Snifters, 8, 9
Strainers, 5, 6
Straws, 5

Tahiti. *See* Polynesia
Techniques, 37
Thailand, 69, 114
Tiki bowls, 9
Tiki couture (dressing/styling
    a cocktail), 13

Tiki mugs, 10, 132
Tools, bartender, 5–7
Trader Vic's, 1
Traverse City, MI, 62

Virgin Islands, settlement and
    importance of, 63
Volcano bowls, 162, 165

About the Authors

LYNN CALVO, an acclaimed restaurant and bar designer, began her tiki journey after traveling the globe and later catering tiki-inspired events throughout the Hamptons and East End of Long Island from a sunset-orange truck outfitted with a thatched tiki bar. Her infusions and mobile island paradise became an overnight sensation, so she opened Lynn's Hula Hut, a Polynesian-style tiki bar in Montauk, New York, where she lives and where locals and visitors alike crowd the bar for the best drinks around.

JAMES O. FRAIOLI is an award-winning cookbook author with 20 cookbooks to his name, including *Culinary Birds*, winner of a 2014 James Beard Award. His titles have been featured on the Food Network and *Ellen* and have appeared on dozens of national radio shows, including *Martha Stewart Living Radio*. They have also received praise from publications such as *Forbes Traveler*, the *New York Times*, *Reader's Digest*, and the *San Francisco Chronicle*. He lives in Redmond, Washington.